KNOWLEDGE AND REALITY IN NINE QUESTIONS

D1611091

ALSO AVAILABLE FROM BLOOMSBURY

Critical Thinking, Robert Arp and Jamie Carlin Watson

Epistemology: The Key Thinkers, edited by Stephen Hetherington

Everyday Examples, David Cunning

How to Win Every Argument, Madsen Pirie

Problems in Epistemology and Metaphysics, edited by Steven B. Cowan

KNOWLEDGE AND REALITY IN NINE QUESTIONS

A First Book in Philosophy

MATTHEW DAVIDSON

BLOOMSBURY ACADEMIC
LONDON • NEW YORK • OXFORD • NEW DELHI • SYDNEY

BLOOMSBURY ACADEMIC
Bloomsbury Publishing Plc
50 Bedford Square, London, WC1B 3DP, UK
1385 Broadway, New York, NY 10018, USA

BLOOMSBURY, BLOOMSBURY ACADEMIC and the Diana logo are
trademarks of Bloomsbury Publishing Plc

First published in Great Britain 2021

Cover design by Jason Anscomb

A catalogue record for this book is available from the British Library.

A catalog record for this book is available from the Library of Congress.

ISBN: HB: 978-1-3501-6142-9
       PB: 978-1-3501-6143-6
       ePDF: 978-1-3501-6144-3
       eBook: 978-1-3501-6145-0

Typeset by RefineCatch Limited, Bungay, Suffolk

To find out more about our authors and books visit www.bloomsbury.com
and sign up for our newsletters.

For my first philosophy teachers:
Hugh Chandler, Robert McKim, and Frederick Schmitt.

CONTENTS

HOW TO USE THIS BOOK

This book is intended as a first book in philosophy, with a focus on questions in metaphysics and epistemology. The idea is that this is a book that a philosopher can hand to someone with little or no training in philosophy and convey to her some of what it is that philosophers do and care about, and why.

I've chosen to focus on nine topics in metaphysics and epistemology. There are, of course, many topics worthy of being covered an introductory book of this sort. I chose these because they are in my experience of particular interest to non-philosophers. I also always have really admired Bertrand Russell's *The Problems of Philosophy* from 1912, and this book—though very different in many respects from *Problems*—is written with that book in mind.

It is my suspicion that many secondary introductory philosophy books are written for two audiences: students and professional philosophers. This often means that the "introductory" book is simply too hard for someone with no training in philosophy to pick up and understand. If I'm writing a book with professional philosophers in mind, and I'm giving an overview of a particular issue; I will feel pressure to lay out completely the conceptual terrain. But the conceptual terrain in most important and interesting philosophical issues is incredibly complex, with multiple views and replies to each and modifications in light of the replies, and so on. It is very easy for those without philosophical training to get lost in the weeds.

It is my principal concern that the reader of the book *do* some philosophy in the course of reading it. So, I do try to give some idea of the conceptual and dialectical background to various philosophical issues, but I don't try to do so exhaustively. This is precisely what I— and I suspect most philosophers—do in an introduction to philosophy class. In such a class, I want the students to get some feel for a philosophical issue and to grasp some of the debate that arises around that particular issue. If I do that, I've succeeded. In this book, I adopt positions and argue for them, but I do so intentionally leaving out many counterarguments that might be mounted to the sort of line I take. Rather, at the end of each chapter I refer the first-time reader of philosophy to further resources that will provide further thinking on the issues I cover.

ACKNOWLEDGMENTS

I am grateful to the many students I have had in introduction to philosophy over my nearly twenty years at California State University, San Bernardino. It has been a joy to do philosophy with them in the context of small-class settings. I also am grateful to my teachers, friends, and colleagues over the years, who helped me to be in a place where I could write this book. These include: Frederick Schmitt, Robert McKim, Hugh Chandler, Alvin Plantinga, Alan Sidelle, Dean Zimmerman, Mike Byrd, Darcy Otto, Tom Crisp, David Suryk, Rachel Siordia, Edward Wierenga, James Van Cleve, and Tony Roy. I am especially grateful to Gordon Barnes, who through many conversations over the years has extensively shaped the way I see the project of doing philosophy. For comments on drafts of chapters of the book, I thank Dan Korman, Dan Speak, Brandon Johns, Gordon Barnes, Tony Roy, James Van Cleve, Steven Cahn, and David Friedell, and several anonymous reviewers. They made the book better than it would have been otherwise. Colleen Coalter, my editor at Bloomsbury has been incredibly helpful, including in selecting a title for the book. I am most grateful to my family: Claudia, Harold, Mark, and Renee.

Introduction

A BIT ABOUT PHILOSOPHY

So, you're reading this short work of philosophy. A reasonable question at the beginning is: What exactly *is* this philosophy that I'm reading about? In many introduction to philosophy courses one starts with the meaning of the word "philosophy." The word "philosophy" originally (roughly 2,500 years ago in ancient Greece) comes from the Greek word *philosophia*, which means something like "love of wisdom." But this is just a start; it doesn't tell you, for instance, what philosophy is as it is done today. (And, while we're at it; it doesn't tell you very much about what philosophy as it was done by the ancient Greeks like Plato and Aristotle, either.)

I think the best place to start in understanding what philosophy is, is to look at some of the questions philosophers study (some of which we will take up later in the book!) and note how they differ from similar-appearing questions people in other disciplines study.

Some Questions Philosophers Ask

1   What makes an action right or wrong?

2   What makes a society a just society?

3   What is it to know that a statement is true?

4   I think that I live in a world with tables, chairs, dogs, other people, and the like. How do I know that I'm not completely wrong in these beliefs?

5   Do numerals like "2" and "4" refer to anything? That is, do they function like the name "Michelle Obama" does in referring to something—the woman Michelle Obama?

6   What is the difference between science and non-science?

7   What sort of thing am I? Am I made of matter? Am I some other kind of thing?

8   What is it to have free will?

9   What is time?

10 If there is a perfectly good, all-powerful, all-knowing being; why is there evil?

Contrast these philosophical questions with similar-sounding topics a non-philosopher might investigate. A sociologist or anthropologist or social psychologist may tell us what we believe about what makes a society just, which things we believe to be science or non-science, and what kind of thing we believe ourselves to be. A theologian may tell us what particular Muslims or Christians or Jews believe about why God allows evil. But a philosopher asks what the true answers to questions like the ten questions above are.

You may be thinking: "That's all well and good; those are philosophical questions. But what *is* philosophy? What makes them philosophical questions?" (This would be a well-put philosophical question, by the way!) Some philosophers think that philosophy should be in some sense continuous with science and it exists to help the scientist in her scientific endeavors. This is a relatively recent view of philosophy, which has its roots in the work of David Hume in the eighteenth century; and has received a careful articulation only in the last seventy-five years or so in the work of people like the American philosopher W.V. Quine.

There is a much older view of philosophy, and this is what has been and continues to be the dominant view of the nature of the discipline. This view goes back nearly 2,500 years to ancient Greek philosophers like Plato and Aristotle. According to this perspective, philosophy tries to tell us about the fundamental nature of reality and how we know about it. Now, this isn't all that philosophy does according to this tradition. But it is very important that it do these two things.

I myself fall into the older camp on the nature of philosophy, and this book will proceed as though the principal task of the philosopher is to investigate the fundamental nature of reality (which is called "metaphysics") and how it is that we know about this reality (which is called "epistemology.") Thus, in this book the questions we seek to understand and see how one might answer are broadly questions of metaphysics or epistemology.

You will notice many distinctive features of philosophy as we do some philosophy throughout the course of the book. First, philosophers care a great deal about *arguments*. We want to know if arguments are good, or not. There are some terms philosophers use when they assess arguments. It is good to learn them. An *argument* is a series of statements (*premises*) that are intended to support another statement (*conclusion*). A *valid* argument is an argument that is such that its premises can't be true while its conclusion is false. (Though a valid argument may have false premises.) A *sound* argument is a valid argument with true premises. (Can you see why any sound argument has to have a true conclusion?) Note also: *Arguments* are valid/invalid, sound/unsound; *parts of arguments* (premises/conclusions) are true or false.

Second, you may notice that philosophers are very concerned with being clear and with drawing distinctions. A great deal of philosophical progress has come out of clarifying the terms and concepts used in common philosophical debates. Third, you also may notice that things that seem obvious to non-philosophers don't always seem obvious to us philosophers. Philosophers try to ask questions of assumptions that may seem obvious to most people.

Finally, you will notice that philosophers often appeal to philosophical intuitions. You might think of the role of intuitions in philosophical reasoning as similar to the role of intuitions in mathematical reasoning. If I am doing a mathematical proof, at times I just intuitively "see" that certain claims in the proof have to be true. Perhaps the clearest instance of this might be at the level of axioms (the starting points of the proof), which may seem self-evidently true. I rely on my mathematical intuitions in the course of the proof to assure that I have not gone wrong in my mathematical reasoning: Do the axioms of the proof have to be true? Does this subsequent step in the proof have to be true given the previous steps in the proof? Something similar happens in the course of philosophical reasoning. I will use my philosophical intuitions to see whether claims that purport to have to be true actually have to be true.

These intuitions often are apparent in the philosopher's use of *thought experiments*. Thought experiments are common in philosophical reasoning, and they may strike the non-philosopher as strange or startling. So we should say a bit about them before we proceed further.

Thought Experiments

In the course of doing philosophy, philosophers come up with possible scenarios that often are incredibly unlikely to happen, and sometimes which may strike the layperson as bizarre. We call these scenarios "thought experiments." They are something like the experiments of the scientist in that they allow us to test philosophical theories to see if they hold up. But unlike those of the scientist, these experiments are purely mental and imaginative in their construction. For instance, here is a famous thought experiment that will give you some indication of what I'm talking about. As you read it, ask yourself: Would you be willing to go in the Experience Machine?

The Experience Machine (from Robert Nozick): Suppose there were a machine that I could hook up to that would give me any experience I wanted to have. So while connected to the machine I might experience that I am an ancient Roman emperor, with experiences of all the trappings of that position. The machine could make me forget about the way things actually are, so that I'm not worrying about things like the health of those I love or the state of the nation I live in. The machine has life-support systems that allow me to stay on it indefinitely. Suppose after realizing that I enjoy my experiences on the machine better than those off, I decide never to disconnect. While I'm on the machine, bad things happen to things I care about (my family, my friends, my nation, etc.). But I'm totally unaware of this, as I think I'm a (benevolent and wise!) Roman emperor.

Obviously, there is no such machine. Perhaps there may be in the distant future, but there isn't now. Perhaps there never will be such a device. But there *could* be. What is the purpose of the example, then? Nozick uses it to try to answer a number of related philosophical questions. Nozick's main focus is refuting a view called *hedonism*: The view that the good life consists in having pleasurable experiences and avoiding pain. We will focus on a more general question raised by the Experience Machine: *Is what is important how things actually are, or how we experience the way things are?* You might ask why we need a fanciful example like the Experience Machine to answer this question. We could just note that sometimes if we don't experience things as they are, later on we can suffer negative consequences. Thus, clearly how things actually are—and not just how we experience them to be—is important.

But what the thought experiment allows us to do is control for factors that might cause us to give wrong answers to this philosophical question. This controlling for confounding factors is conceptually like that of the scientific experimenter's doing the same. Suppose I'm a corporate executive, and I believe that I'm very skilled with dealing with subordinates. I believe that I'm a kind and thoughtful boss. In reality, I'm a petty dictator at the office. I'm able to maintain the illusion that I'm a good boss because my subordinates are afraid to tell me their true feelings. This misperception holds, until one time I'm sued for mistreating an employee. Then suddenly the way I actually *am* as a corporate boss matters.

In Nozick's case, though, we can arrange things so that reality doesn't catch up to the person in question. I can go on the Experience Machine and have experiences as though I am a magnanimous boss even if in reality I'm a terrible one. And the machine can give me experiences that never include negative consequences from my misperception of my own managerial qualities. Now we can focus *just* on the question: Irrespective of consequences for me, is what is important here how things *are*, or how I experience them to me to be?

Often times thought experiments arise as counterexamples to a philosophical thesis. For instance, the Experience Machine example often is used as a counterexample to theories of the good that say that what is important *vis-à-vis* my good is what sorts of experiences I have. But how does a strange, even science-fiction sort of example bear on the actual truth of philosophical claim? The answer lies in the nature of philosophical claims. Philosophical claims are generally necessarily true if true. (That 2+2=4 and that all squares have four sides are examples of necessary truths.) We of course want to know whether, for instance, what I'm *actually* obligated to do is maximize pleasure over pain for everyone affected by my actions. Suppose, though, that we can show that this claim is possibly false: We imagine a possible case with a sadist whose pleasure in hurting others outweighs the pain he causes them. It follows from this that I'm *not actually* obligated to maximize pleasure for everyone affected by my actions. (What I'm obligated to do might coincide with maximizing pleasure for all involved, but it's not obligatory *because* it does so.) Thought experiments allow us to assess the *actual* truth of philosophical claims by testing them to see if they are *possibly* false, or perhaps possibly true. If they are possibly false, then the philosophical claim is actually false; and if possibly true, then the philosophical claim is actually true. Thought experiments are a primary source of evidence for and against philosophical theses and theories.

Philosophy, then, looks a bit like science and a bit like mathematics. It is like science in that we do experiments, of a sort—*thought* experiments. It is like mathematics in that we deal principally with necessary truths. But it is clearly distinct from each in its approach and subject matter, as you will see.

There is one other thing I should flag in this front chapter. It is that philosophers agree on very little. (Philosophers disagree on what philosophy itself is, and even on how much we agree!) I'm going to argue for substantive philosophical positions in this book. In some cases they are views not held by a majority, or even a plurality of philosophers. Don't look at this book as supplying "the right answers" to various philosophical questions, in the way a teacher's edition to a text in calculus might. Rather, think of it as an opportunity to think philosophically about some of the most important philosophical questions philosophers have asked during the 2,500-year life of Western philosophy. Your philosophical intuitions may differ from mine, and that's OK! We'll work through the questions and issues that arise in doing so together. I hope this will result in two things. First, that you will get some experience of what it's like to do philosophy as contemporary philosophers do philosophy. Second, that you will emerge with better understanding of the conceptual lay of the land around these questions.

We turn to a series of these questions now.

Reflection Questions

1 What is an argument?

2 What is it for an argument to be valid?

3 What is it for an argument to be sound?

4 What is a philosophical intuition?

5 What is a thought experiment?

FURTHER READING

For further reading on the nature of philosophy, see George Bealer, "A Theory of the A Priori" (*Philosophical Perspectives,* 1999), Janet Levin "The Evidential Status of Philosophical Intuitions" (*Philosophical Studies*, 2005), and Lawrence BonJour, *In Defense of Pure Reason* (Cambridge, 1998) ch. 1. W.V. Quine discusses his views on the nature of philosophy in many places, but his essay "Epistemology Naturalized" in his *Ontological Relativity* (Columbia, 1969) is a good place to start. Robert Nozick gives the Experience Machine example in his famous book *Anarchy, State, and Utopia* (Basic, 1974). Aristotle can be difficult for the beginner, but his *Categories* are a place to start. Plato is easier for the beginner; one might start with *Euthyphro*.

Question 1

WHAT AM I?

For as long as philosophy has been around, philosophers have asked the question, "what am I?" The answer to this might seem straightforward to you; in my own case, I'm a philosopher, a Californian, an American, a human, a fan of Liverpool Football Club, and so on. But this isn't what philosophers typically mean when they ask this question. What we want to know is, "Fundamentally, *what kind of thing* am I?" That is, at a most basic level of description, what sort of entity am I?

The answers to this question matter. For instance, if I am my body or my brain, then it would seem as though I don't survive into any sort of afterlife. For, my body and brain remain on earth and decompose. If I survive into the afterlife, then I must be the sort of thing that can survive the death of material parts of my body.

In this chapter, I want to consider a variety of answers to the question "what am I?" Some of them will be familiar to you; indeed, some of them may be answers you yourself accept. I should say that this is not an exhaustive list of possible answers. I want to focus on those that have had substantial philosophical support or impact.

Answer One: I am nothing that lasts over time. That is, I don't exist, or exist only for a moment.

The first answer to the question "what am I?" is that I am nothing that persists through time. There are two sorts of views that might lead one to adopt Answer One. First, one might think that there is no self at all. This might seem a strange view to you: "Of course I exist!", you might insist. But many Buddhists think that the self is illusory. It just appears to us that there is a self. Indeed, many Buddhists think the belief in the self is one of the things that keeps us from enlightenment and (thus) salvation.

Philosopher Peter Unger, in an article strikingly titled "I Do Not Exist", argues for Answer One. Unger states that if I did exist, I would be a physical object that has things like cells as parts. But there are no entities with parts. Thus, I don't exist, either. Why think that there aren't any entities that have parts? Because if there were such entities there would be a definite number of parts (like cells) I could remove from any such entity and have it continue in existence; but there is no such definite number. So there aren't any entities with parts.

Second, one may also defend Answer One if one thinks that what "I" refers to when I use it is a momentarily-lasting person stage. What is a momentarily-lasting person stage? It is a person that lasts only for a moment, and in the next moment a new person comes into existence. This is also a view held by many Buddhists.

There is one last view on which one might think that Answer One is correct. David Hume, in his *Treatise of Human Nature* said this about the self:

> I may venture to affirm of the rest of mankind, that they are nothing but a bundle or collection of different perceptions, which succeed each other with an inconceivable rapidity, and are in a perpetual flux and movement ... The mind is a kind of theatre, where several perceptions successively make their appearance; pass, re-pass, glide away, and mingle in an infinite variety of postures and situations. There is properly no simplicity in it at one time, nor identity in different; whatever natural propension we may have to imagine that simplicity and identity.
>
> Book I, Part IV, Section VI

According to Hume, what is the self? It is a bundle of "perceptions"— mental states of various kinds. So, when I use "I" to refer to myself, I refer to a bundle of perceptions. Hume seems to think that each bundle of perceptions has its members essentially. This implies that a bundle ceases to exist when it gains or loses a mental state. So I don't persist through time, as the mental states that I might in ordinary contexts call mine are constantly changing.

It is worth noting that it's not clear what sort of thing a "bundle" is when we talk about bundles of perceptions. In ordinary contexts when we talk about bundles, we mention things like bundles of matches or bundles of flowers. And we may ask of those sorts of cases, (pointing at the matches), "Are there two kinds of things there, in my hand, the bundle and the individual matches? Or are there just the matches?" If we try to list accurately all the different kinds of things in the world, would we include bundles? Or would we include just things like matches, roses, and firewood? However, even if we think that in addition to those matches in my hand there is a bundle of matches, it's not clear what a bundle of *mental states* would be.

Perhaps you're thinking that Hume just could say, "I am *those* mental states" while referring plurally to number of mental states. This won't work, though; for each of us is one thing, and thus can't be identical with many things. (We will give an argument for this in the next chapter.)

Let's set these concerns aside for now. Suppose we can make sense of the idea of bundles of mental states. Is this the sort of thing I am? I don't think so. As the eighteenth-century Scottish philosopher Thomas Reid pointed out in a reply to David Hume's bundle theory; I am a thing that thinks and has opinions and remembers doing things, and no bundle of mental states does that.

Furthermore, it seems pretty clear to me that I exist, and I have existed for multiple decades. If these claims are true, then any version of Answer One has to be wrong. So I'm inclined to think that we should look to other answers to the question of what kind of thing I am. Whatever I am; I am something, something that thinks, and something that persists through change over time.

Answer Two: I am a persisting physical object of some kind.

According to Answer Two, I am something physical or material and I last for more than a moment of time. What kind of physical thing might I be that is like that? Some candidates are: a brain, or a body, or the combination of a brain and a body. Some philosophers think I am a physical object that stands to my body in a way analogous to the way a statue stands to a piece of rock out of which it is carved.

I think that we can show that I am none of these kinds of things. The following may not be a description of how things will be, but it is at least a description of how things *could* be. I die, and after I die my body and brain remain on earth and gradually decompose. Thus my body and brain cease to exist. However, I live on in an afterlife. This afterlife never ends, and in the afterlife I am reacquainted with deceased loved ones and pets.

Perhaps this is not how things are. Perhaps when I die, I cease to exist. But it *could* be that things go this way. (Indeed, many people believe this is what will happen to me after I die.) That this could occur shows that I am neither my brain nor my body. For I may exist even if neither my brain nor my body exists, which implies that I am possibly distinct from brain or my body. And this implies that I am actually distinct from my brain or body. (The reasoning here is somewhat technical, though I supply it in the appendix at the end of the chapter.)

I think that this example also shows that I'm nothing that emerges from my body (or brain) the way a statue emerges from a piece of stone that is carved. For if the stone out of which the statue is made doesn't exist, neither does the statue. Thus, I am not my brain, nor my body, nor something that emerges from my body (or brain).

Answer Three: I am a nonphysical mind.

According to Answer Three, I am a mind—a thinking thing—that isn't made of matter. Philosophers sometimes call such an entity a soul (though there are interesting questions to what extent a philosopher's concept of a soul overlaps with the ordinary concept of a soul). The classic statement of this view is from the seventeenth century mathematician and philosopher René Descartes. In 1641 in his *Meditations on First Philosophy* (a very commonly-used work in English-speaking introduction to philosophy courses), he says

> I have a clear and distinct idea of myself, as far as I am only a thinking and unextended thing, and as, on the other hand, I possess a distinct idea of body, in as far as it is only an extended and unthinking thing, it is certain that I [that is, my mind, by which I am what I am], is entirely and truly distinct from my body, and may exist without it.
>
> DESCARTES 1913, Med. VI

This view has come to be known as mind-body or Cartesian dualism. The term "dualism" comes from the fact that on this view there are two kinds of things, mental things that aren't made of matter or located in space, and physical things that are made of matter and located in space. But it's worth pointing out that there are versions of Answer Three on which there isn't any matter—only minds. The Irish philosopher George Berkeley, who was born thirty-five years after Descartes died, had a view like this. (We will examine his view in chapter 9.)

It is worth noting that this view of what I am may fit well with the intuition that I could survive the death of my body and exist in some sort of afterlife. If I am a nonphysical mind, it is not implausible to think that I am the sort of thing that isn't dependent on a body or brain for its existence. My body and brain may decay and cease to exist, and I live on. Currently my mind may interact with my body, but this does not need to be the case. If the afterlife story we stated above is correct, it won't always be the case.

Answer Four: I am a combination of an immaterial mind and a body.

On Answer Four, I have two parts—an immaterial mind and physical body. My physical body is located in space (currently in a chair at a table). My immaterial mind interacts with my body; events in my body cause events in my mind and conversely. This might be an attractive answer if one is concerned with the fact that we often speak as though we are material objects. If Maria asks José to describe himself, he might say that he is 2 meters tall and weighs 85 kilograms. This would not be an unusual-sounding answer. But if José is an immaterial mind that isn't located in space, what he has said is false. Now, the body that his mind interacts with is 2 meters tall and weighs 85 kilograms. But that's not him; he's the mind. And the body isn't even a *part* of him. Thus, on Answer Three one might be concerned that these sorts of claims about properties I have turn out to be false. But on Answer Four, we could reply that there are two parts of José, and one part of him is 2 meters tall and weighs 85 kilograms. So on Answer Four we're closer to saying something true with these sorts of claims.

But Answer Four encounters the same sorts of difficulties that Answer Two does. What is the difference between a view on which I am an immaterial mind that causally (that is, in the sense of "cause and effect") interacts with a body; and the view on which I am something with two parts, an immaterial mind and a body?

Presumably it must be that in the latter case I have both the body and immaterial mind essentially. Otherwise, the two views seem to collapse into each other. But if on Answer Four I have a body essentially, then I can't exist without my body. But, as we saw above, I can exist without my body. Thus, Answer Four cannot be correct.

Conclusion

What am I, then? If I may exist and my body or brain not exist, then I'm neither of those. Whatever I am, I am some sort of thinking thing—a mind of some sort. Thus, the best candidate here is that I am an immaterial mind of the sort that Descartes thought he was. That is, I think that Answer Three is correct.

Appendix: A proof that if it is possible that x≠y, then actually x≠y.

In chapter 2, I argued that I am not my body or brain. This argument relied on an inference from the *possible* distinctness from my body or brain to the *actual* distinctness from my body or brain. This may seem counterintuitive to you. Why would the *possibility* of something have implications for the way things *actually* are? However, identity is a special relation in that possible identity and distinctness claims have implications for identity and distinctness actually.

The reasoning here gets technical, so give yourself time with it. And you still can follow the main reasoning in chapter 2 without all the details of the proof below.

Here's our proof that if it is possible that x≠y, then actually x≠y. Suppose first it is possible that x≠y. Suppose then that x and y exist. We're going to prove that given these first two assumptions, actually x≠y. Next, we invoke a principle called *Leibniz's Law*. The principle is named after the great seventeenth century philosopher and mathematician Gottfried Leibniz. Leibniz's Law is the proposition that if some object A has a property that object B lacks, then A and B are distinct objects (that is, there are two of them). For instance, suppose I own just one automobile, a sedan. Suppose I observe that the vehicle in the parking lot in front of me is a truck. Then I may conclude that the car in front of me isn't my car. My car has a property (*being a sedan*) which the vehicle in front of me lacks. Thus, the vehicle in front of me isn't my car.

From Leibniz's Law, we can derive that actually x≠y. From our first two assumptions (that it is possible that x≠y and that x and y exist), we can see that y actually has the property *possibly being distinct from x*. But x actually lacks the property *possibly being distinct from x* (each thing is necessarily identical with itself). So y has a property x lacks. Thus, via Leibniz's Law, it actually is the case that x≠y. Thus, we have shown that if it is possible that x≠y, that actually x≠y.

Reflection Questions

1 What is the argument given in the chapter that I am not my body or brain?

2 What is Cartesian dualism?

3 What is David Hume's view of the self?

4   What does Thomas Reid say about Hume's view of the self?

5   What kind of thing do you think you are? Why?

FURTHER READING

Classic answers to the question of what sort of thing I am can be found in Descartes' *Meditations on First Philosophy* (in particular Meditations 2 and 6) and David Hume's *Treatise on Human Nature* (Book 1 Part IV Sections 5–6). Excellent contemporary sources include Peter van Inwagen's *Metaphysics* 4th ed. (Routledge, 2018) chs. 10 and 11. Van Inwagen defends a view on which we are material entities. Erik Olson's *What Are We? A Study in Personal Ontology* (Oxford, 2007) gives a good survey of difference answers to the question we focused on in this chapter. Lynne Rudder Baker's important book *Persons and Bodies* (Cambridge, 2000), chs. 4–6 has a defense of a view on which we are material things constituted by our bodies. Brie Gertler's "Can Feminists Be Cartesians?" (*Dialogue 2002*) has a nice discussion of "Cartesian" forms of reasoning, of which this chapter is one. Mayra Schechtman has an interesting discussion of the nature of the self in *The Constitution of Selves* (Cornell, 2007).

Question 2

CAN I ACHIEVE IMMORTALITY THROUGH TECHNOLOGY?

In the last chapter, we asked about the sort of thing I am. In this chapter, we will ask a related question; about the prospect of surviving the death of my body via advanced technology.

Suppose I am ill and have only a few months to live. I don't like the prospect of my ceasing to exist. I say to myself, "The sickness is in my body. My mind is fine. If I could simply switch bodies to one that wasn't diseased, I'd be able to continue with my life." Then I remember this new company that promises to allow one to change bodies. To accomplish this feat, they first make a digital representation of my brain. They then are able to configure another brain such that it is in the same states the copied brain was in. This new brain is placed in another body, connected neurally in the proper manner, and voila! I have a new body. I can leave the diseased one behind.

Is this possible? I don't mean technologically possible. Let's just grant that in the future we will be able to figure out a way to represent digitally all of my brain states and subsequently cause a physical object like a brain to match those states. (I'm not discounting the difficulty of this; the human brain is the most complex entity in the universe, so far as we know. But for the sake of asking and trying to answer particular philosophical questions, we'll assume that in the future we will figure out how to do this.) What I mean is this: If we could figure out the technology, would this be a way of changing bodies? Presumably this could be done many times over a long period of time. Would it then be a way of achieving something like immortality?

Let's fill out the scenario we've started examining. Suppose the scenario goes like this. I lie inside a brain scanner. I am rendered unconscious, and a digital representation of my brain is created. My heart is stopped, and my dead body and brain are cremated. Another brain is placed inside a brain-state-configuration machine, which is a machine that can manipulate the neural states of a brain so that the brain matches the neural configuration of past brains. The brain-state-configuration machine causes the new brain to be structured as my old brain was, leaving out states tied to the specific body I had (like remembering I have a scar on my arm), and perhaps states that give rise to things like mental illness and other sorts of sufferings. The new brain is placed in a new body and is connected to the new body neurally. The scientists performing the operation cause the person (we'll call him "Newman") with the new brain and body to wake up.

What would things look like from Newman's perspective? What would he say happened? Presumably, he'd say that he used to have a diseased body, but through advanced technology now has a new body and brain. If we asked him who he was, he'd say that he is me—

Davidson. If we asked him what he was for Halloween when he was five, he'd give the same answer I would give—a vampire. If we asked him who his parents are, he'd give the same answer I would give. And so on.

Is Newman right? Is he me? This will turn out to be a more difficult question to answer than you might have thought at first. Let us first try to get clear on what we're asking when we ask "is Newman me?" We aren't asking if Newman is *like* me. We already have an answer to that: Mentally he is a lot like me, and physically he isn't (he has a different body). Rather, we are asking if Newman and I are the *same person*; whether in our scenario there is one person with two names, "Newman" and "Davidson." Think of cases where there is one person with two names: "Mark Twain" and "Samuel Clemens", "Jay-Z" and "Shawn Carter", or even "Superman" and "Clark Kent." In each case there really is *one* person that we're talking about. If Samuel Clemens committed a crime, it would be proper to hold Mark Twain accountable for it—after all, they're the same person. Or, suppose we want to count how many things there are. We do so by writing down a name of each thing and writing a number next to it, like so:

1   Mt. Everest

2   Australia

3   Tokyo

4   Pope Francis

    etc.

(So Mt. Everest is the first object on our list, Australia the second, etc.) If we put both "Davidson" and "Newman" on the list, we'd be double counting. The number we had written next to the last item on the list would be at least one higher than the actual number of things there are.

Then, in this sense of "is the same person as", are Davidson and Newman the same person? Answering this question will depend on what *sort* of thing I am. Suppose I am something like a brain or body or animal. Then it is hard to see how I survive if my body is destroyed but my mental states are transferred to another body. For the sake of our discussion here, though, let's grant that I am some sort of thing the identity of which is closely tied to the continuation of mental states. (So maybe I am an immaterial mind or soul as we argued in the last chapter, or maybe I am some sort of bundle of mental states.)

Let us return to the brain scanning scenario, with a slight change. Suppose I have my brain scanned, and my body is cremated. But suppose the scientists doing the procedure are friends of mine, and they like me. So rather than the brain-state-configuration machine configuring one brain like mine, it configures two brains—inside two distinct bodies—like mine. This results in two persons. Let's call one of these persons "Newman1" and the other "Newman2." Suppose Newman1 and Newman2 are put in separate rooms and are brought to consciousness after the experiment. The scientists ask Newman1 the same questions asked of Newman in the first experimental scenario. Newman1 gives the same answers: He'd say he's Davidson. He'd say he was a vampire for Halloween when he was five etc. Now, the scientists go into the other room and ask the same questions of Newman2. He gives the same answers Newman1 gives. He says he's Davidson, and that he was a vampire for Halloween when he was five. And so on.

But now we have a problem. I can't be both Newman1 and Newman2. In fact, more generally, I (one thing) can't be two things. That's impossible. Each thing is necessarily identical with itself and nothing else. In fact, we can give an argument that I can't be both Newman1 and Newman2. Start with the fact that we know that Newman1≠Newman2. Why? Because Newman1 is in one room, and Newman2 in another. Suppose that Davidson=Newman1 and Davidson=Newman2. Then because identity is transitive (if a=b and b=c, then a=c) we can derive that Newman1=Newman2. But this is false; Newman1≠Newman2. So I can't be both Newman1 and Newman2.

Maybe I am *either* Newman1 *or* Newman2, then. But that seems purely arbitrary. I stand in the same relevant relations to Newman1 and Newman2. Each has a brain that has been configured in the way my brain was configured before the procedure. How could it be that I am Newman1 rather than Newman2; or Newman2 rather than Newman1?

The right answer seems to be that I am neither Newman1 nor Newman2. That is, I don't survive the procedure. So, perhaps what I should do is make sure that more than one brain isn't configured in the way that my brain was. If there is more than one candidate for being me after the surgery, I don't survive. But if there is just one, I would survive. Right?

Wrong, it seems to me. I bear the same relevant relations to Newman1 and Newman2. Each has a brain configured in the way my brain was configured. If we say I survive so long as there aren't two contenders for being me post-operation, we are saying that my survival as Newman1 depends on the existence of Newman2. But surely whether I am Newman1 has only to do with facts about me, Davidson, and Newman1.

Let's change the scenario a bit to try to make clearer this objection to the view that I survive so long as post-scanning there is only one contender for being me. Suppose that my brain is scanned and the configuration stored in a computer. It is to be used to reconfigure a brain to match mine. However, before the procedure can be done, hackers on the other side of the world break in and steal copies of the data that holds my brain configuration. They do nothing with the data, however. Further, no one other than the people who stole the data are aware of the theft. Now, locally a brain is configured using the brain-state-configuration machine to be like my brain. A new individual results, whom we can call Newman1. All is good, right? I survive the procedure on this view, because there is just one contender for being me.

But suppose that rather than doing nothing with the data, the hackers on the other side of the world use their own brain-state-configuration machine to configure another brain to be like my brain. Suppose further that they do so at the same time as the configuration of the brain locally. Each brain is put into a new body, and the resulting people are awakened at the same time. Call the new person locally "Newman1," (just as we did before); and call the new person on the other side of the world "Newman2." The view under consideration—that I survive so long as there is just one candidate for being me after the procedure—tells us that I don't survive the procedure. There are two candidates for being me— Newman1 and Newman2. But surely the existence of Newman2 on the other side of the world can't affect whether I survive as Newman1.

If I am Newman1 in the single case, I should be Newman1 even if Newman2 happens to exist on the other side of the world. All the same relevant relations between Newman1 and me continue to hold in the case where Newman2 also is created.

Then it looks false that I survive the procedure if and only if there is one best candidate for being me. Thus, it looks like I don't survive the procedure at all. If uploading oneself into a computer and downloading oneself into a new body works in the way we're imagining, I don't survive the procedure. Someone a lot like me may survive. And that may be some comfort to me, in the way that having my children survive me might be. But it's not a way for me to achieve immortality.

Reflection Questions

1   In popular depictions involving the sort of science-fiction cases detailed in this chapter, what are we supposed to think happens?

2   Why might one think that in the first scenario that I am Newman? (Hint: What does Newman say about who Newman is?)

3   Why can't I be both Newman1 and Newman2?

4   What should we say about my survival in the cases with Newman1 and Newman2?

5   What does this imply for my survival in the normal science-fiction download case?

FURTHER READING

The most important contemporary discussion of questions of personal identity (which form the core of the discussion in this chapter) is Derek Parfit's *Reasons and Persons* (Oxford, 1986). There are several anthologies devoted to issues in personal identity. John Perry's *Personal Identity* (California, 2008) is a good collection of sources with a focus on the historical debate. Amélie Oksenberg Rorty's *The Identities of Persons* (California, 1976) also is a good collection of sources on the debate through the mid-70s. Raymond Martin and John Barresi's *Personal Identity* (Blackwell, 2002) contains overall more contemporary (and difficult) selections. Lynne Rudder Baker's book *Persons and Bodies: A Constitution View* (Cambridge, 2000) has further discussion of questions of personal identity.

Question 3

WHAT IF I CAN'T TELL IF I'M IN THE MATRIX?

The year 1999 saw the release of the movie *The Matrix*. It is set some time close to the year 2199. In it, human beings exist in vats of liquid, and these vats are collected together in great colonies. The humans' brains are connected to computers that give them experiences as though they are living ordinary lives in (what looks to be) Chicago in the late-twentieth century. As a result they believe they are living ordinary lives in urban America in the late-twentieth century.

The movie has caused many people to ask this question: How do I know I am not like the characters in the Matrix? In particular, how do I know I'm not in a vat of liquid, being fed information by a computer in such a way that my beliefs about how things are around me are mostly false? More generally, how do I know my beliefs about the world aren't radically false? I think that I'm in Southern California in the early part of the twenty-first century, that there are other people around me with whom I interact, and so on. But I *could* be wrong in these beliefs. Does this possibility keep me from having knowledge from them?

Maybe you're thinking: OK, it's possible that I'm one of a great number of humans in vats of liquid being fed information by a computer, and that my beliefs about the external world are mostly false. But this is really very improbable. So why should I worry about it? Why does the mere possibility that I am in a vat of liquid being fed information by a computer have anything to do with whether I should be skeptical of what I previously thought was knowledge of the external world?

This is a good question! Here's the problem, though. It looks like I can't tell from my experience whether I'm in a Matrix-like situation or not. If I were one of many humans in a great colony of vats being fed information by a computer, then I wouldn't know, for instance, that right now there are other people around me in a university setting. This is because if I know something, then that thing I know is true. And I can't tell I'm not in a Matrix-like situation. Maybe I am! If I were, things would look just as they do right now. And if I can't tell from my experience whether I am in a vat being fed information by a computer or not, then I can't know there are people around me in a university setting right now.

Let's put these notions into an explicit argument. We will call this the *Matrix Argument*.

(Premise 1) If I know I am in a university setting surrounded by students, then I am able to tell I am not in a great colony of vats being fed information by a computer.

(Premise 2) I am not able to tell I'm not in a great colony of vats being fed information by a computer.

(Conclusion) Therefore, I don't know I am in a university setting surrounded by students.

Now, I just picked the claim that I'm in a university setting surrounded by students at random. We could have picked that I'm sitting in a chair, that I'm typing at a computer, or the like. So we should think of the argument as an argument for a thoroughgoing skepticism about the external world. If this is a good argument, I would have much less knowledge than I thought I had.

What should we make of the Matrix Argument? First, we can note that it is valid; that is, if its premises are true, then its conclusion has to be true. To see this, consider its form:

1 If I know that p, then I am able to tell whether q.

2 I am not able to tell whether q.

3 Therefore, I don't know that p.

("Where "p" abbreviates, "I know I am in a university setting surrounded by students;" and "q" abbreviates, "I am able to tell I am not in a great colony of vats being fed information by a computer."")"

Because it's valid; if we want to reject its conclusion, we need to reject at least one of the premises. Are its premises true? Let's start with the second premise. Why might someone think that it is true? Well, suppose I were in a vat of liquid being fed information by a computer as in the Matrix. How would things look to me? They wouldn't look as though I'm in a vat (this is assured by the way the scenario is set up in the movie). They'd look exactly as they do right now. It would appear as though I were sitting in a chair and there were university students around me, and the like. Then it looks like I simply can't tell if I'm in a Matrix-like situation or not. Things would look like this either way. This gives strong support to the second premise.

What about the first premise? Return to the claim that if I know something, that something I know is true. (I can't know something false, though I might firmly believe it is true.) Thus, if I know I am in a university setting surrounded by students, then it is true I am in a university setting surrounded by students. Thus, if I know I am in a university setting surrounded by students, I am not in a colony of vats being fed information by a computer. So, my being so-envatted is inconsistent with my knowing I am in a university setting surrounded by students. Then one might think that in order to know that I am in a university setting surrounded by students, I need to be able to tell whether or not I am in a colony of vats being fed information by a computer. This last claim is our second premise. Thus, we have reason for thinking the second premise is true.

Should we then think that I don't know that I am in a university setting, surrounded by students? Or that I'm sitting in a chair? Or much else I thought I knew about the world? This would be implied by the soundness of the Matrix Argument. First, we must consider replies to the argument. We will focus on a reply to each premise. Each reply purports to show that a premise of the argument is false.

Let us begin once again with the second premise. In his *Proof of An External World*, twentieth century British philosopher G.E. Moore argues that he does know ordinary claims about the world. He imagines holding up a hand while saying "here is a hand," and holding up another hand while saying "here is another [hand]." He insists that he knows both of these propositions. And he knows that his knowing them implies that he has knowledge of the external world. So skepticism about knowledge of the external world has to be false.

We could imagine someone in the vein of Moore saying, with respect to Premise 2; that they *are able to tell* whether they're in a Matrix situation. "Look around! Here is a table. Here are some students. Here is a university building. I absolutely am able to tell I'm not in a colony of vats being fed information by a computer!" So we can imagine someone following Moore's example and insisting that Premise 2 is false.

It might seem to you that Moore isn't taking the skeptical argument seriously. He's asserting, rather than giving detailed arguments, that he knows things that we don't know if the argument is sound. Isn't he doing something very close to just denying the conclusion of the skeptic's argument? Surely there is something wrong with this way of replying to the skeptic.

I have sympathy for this concern. But we could imagine someone with Moorean sympathies saying something like the following. "However compelling I find the premises of the argument, I find the denial of its conclusion far more compelling. I am pretty certain I know that I'm sitting at a desk writing right now. I am far more sure of this than I am that I can't tell if I am in a colony of vats being fed images by a computer. So faced with a choice between accepting Premise 2, or accepting that I know ordinary claims about the world around me; I should deny Premise 2."

You will have to decide for yourself whether you think that the Moorean strategy is fair to the person putting forth our skeptical argument. There is significant disagreement among philosophers as to whether it is.

The Moorean strategy is not the only way to reply to the argument, though. One also can deny Premise 1. To see how this might be done, let's turn to an example from the contemporary epistemologist Alvin Goldman.

Goldman imagines the following scenario. There are people driving through the countryside, and they are naming objects. They say, "There's a fence. There's a tree. There's a house." And so on. They are able to see well all the objects they name; the lighting is good, their eyesight is fine, and the objects aren't far from the road. They come upon a barn (there are many of them in the countryside) and say, "there's a barn." As they do this, they form the belief that there is a barn in front of them. Do they know there is a barn in front of them? Intuitively we want to say they do, apart from the sorts of skeptical scenarios we've been considering here.

Goldman then modifies this first scenario. (Keep in mind, though, Goldman is *not* a skeptic.) He supposes that most of the rest of the objects in the countryside that look like barns are actually barn façades. These are designed to look like barns from the road, but in reality don't have sides or a roof. One can know that they aren't real barns by walking around them and seeing that they aren't. (Why might someone erect barn façades in the countryside? Perhaps the farmers there are prideful and want to be seen as owning many barns.) Other than the addition of the barn façades, we keep the original scenario just as it was. In particular—and this is important—the object that they are looking at actually is a barn. It is the only barn-appearing object in the area that actually is a barn. Also—and this is also important—they aren't aware of the presence of barn façades in the area. They assume all the things that look like barns are barns. Of this second scenario, Goldman asks: Do they know they're looking at a barn (as they know in the original scenario)? Goldman says they *don't* know they are looking at a barn.

One way in which they might not know they are looking at a barn is if they aren't actually looking at a barn. If they're looking at a barn façade, then of course they don't know they are looking at a barn. But in the second scenario (the fake barn scenario) Goldman presents, they *are* looking at a barn. So why don't they know they are? Goldman says that the presence of the barn façades in the area makes relevant the possibility that what they are looking at isn't an actual barn. As a result, they need to rule out that they aren't looking at a barn façade in order to know they are looking at a barn. How might they do this? They could walk around the front of the object and make sure that it is a real barn.

Maybe you're wondering why they need to check to make sure it is a barn in this second (fake barn) scenario. It is not as though they have any reason to believe it isn't a barn. They weren't, for instance, told by a reliable person that there are many barn façades in the area. But this is not necessary to affect their ability to know, Goldman argues. His reasoning is something like this: If one were to pick from the general area an object that looks like a barn from the road at random, it would be much more likely that the object picked would be a barn façade rather than an actual barn. In some sense, then, it is a matter of luck that the belief that they are looking at a barn is true. So, the presence of the fake barns makes the possibility that the thing that they're looking at is a barn façade relevant. They then need to be able to rule out this possibility.

Goldman draws a general lesson from the example. (Others, like Gail Stine, have drawn the same lesson.) In order to know that some proposition p is true, I don't need to be able to rule out *all* possibilities in which my belief p is false. I need to be able to rule out only *relevant* possibilities in which my belief is false. What is it for a possibility to be relevant? We don't actually have an account of this from Goldman. But we have some sort of grasp of what relevance is in this case. In the first scenario, the possibility that I'm looking at a fake barn isn't relevant. In the second it is. What has changed? One thing is that it is substantially more likely that the object I believe is a barn isn't a barn.

How is this germane to the question of skepticism, and in particular to the truth of Premise 1? Premise 1 says that to know I'm in a university setting surrounded by students I need to be able to rule out the possibility that I am in a colony of vats of liquid being fed information by a computer. But why do I need to be able to rule out that possibility? If Goldman is right, I need to be able to rule out this possibility only if it is relevant. And it is relevant only if it is something that sometimes happens, or is likely to happen, or the like. So, if reality isn't this way—if it doesn't involve skeptical scenarios such as those depicted in *The Matrix*—then I can have knowledge. The mere possibility of these doesn't preclude my knowing that I am in a university setting surrounded by students.

If we want to reject the conclusion of the Matrix Argument, we're going to need to reject at least one of its premises. So, we're going to have to say either that I can have knowledge of the external world without being able to tell if a skeptical scenario holds; or I actually am able to tell that such a scenario doesn't hold. When we looked at a

Moorean response to Premise 2, we imagined Moore saying that he needs to weigh the plausibility of that premise against the plausibility of the denial of the conclusion of the Matrix Argument. We can take this approach with respect to both of the premises of the Matrix Argument. We need to ask: is it more plausible that the premises and conclusion of the Matrix Argument are true; or that the conclusion and thus at least one of the premises is false? It seems to me clear that the latter is more plausible. So which premise should one reject? I find Goldman's reasoning about Premise 1 of the Matrix Argument compelling. So I'm inclined to reject Premise 1. But you may disagree with me on this. You may find Moorean sort of reasoning with respect to Premise 2 more plausible. Or you may think that Premise 1 and Premise 2 are pretty clearly true, and as a result we should accept the conclusion of the Matrix Argument. I myself am quite certain the conclusion is false, and this leads me to reject one of the premises—Premise 1—in the manner of Alvin Goldman.

Reflection Questions

1   What is the skeptical scenario described in the movie *The Matrix*?

2   What is "The Matrix Argument?"

3   What is a reply to the Matrix Argument from G.E. Moore?

4   What is a reply to the Matrix Argument from Alvin Goldman?

5   Which is a better reply to the Matrix Argument? Do you think the Matrix Argument is sound?

FURTHER READING

Arguments with the form of the Matrix Argument are pretty common in the literature. One place you might start is in the first chapter of *Ignorance* (Oxford, 1975). By Peter Unger. The exchange between Fred Dretske (who holds a view similar to Goldman's) and John Hawthorne in *Contemporary Debates in Epistemology* also is illuminating. A third thing to look at is Steven Luper's article "Cartesian Skepticism" in the *Routledge Companion to Epistemology* (2013). The ideas from Alvin Goldman I discuss in the chapter are from his famous paper "Discrimination and Perceptual Knowledge" (*Journal of Philosophy*, 1976). Another classic paper about issues raised in the Matrix Argument (particularly with the first premise) is Gail Stine's "Skepticism, Relevant Alternatives, and Deductive Closure" (*Philosophical Studies,* 1976). She also argues that we only need to rule out relevant possibilities in with our belief is false in order to have knowledge. Moore gives his "refutation of skepticism" in "Proof of an External World" in his *Selected Writings* ed. Thomas Baldwin (Routledge, 1993).

Question 4

WHAT IS IT TO ACT WITH FREE WILL?

From the Scientific Revolution in the seventeenth century until about 100 years ago, many scientists and philosophers thought that *determinism* was true of the universe. What does that mean? It means that they thought that given the laws of nature and total state of the universe in the past, only one future is possible. Determinism implies that given the laws of nature and the total state of the universe long before my birth—10,000,000 years ago, say—it was not possible for me not to have typed the sentence I'm currently typing. Indeed, if determinism is true, given the laws of nature and the total state of the universe in the past; nothing that occurs now could fail to occur.

Note that determinism is different from *fate* as fate typically is depicted in classic literature. Consider the case of Oedipus in the ancient Greek play *Oedipus Rex* by Sophocles. In it, Oedipus is fated to kill his father and sleep with his mother. There is nothing he can do to change the fact that he will do both of these things. He has some control over the circumstances in which these events happen. But regardless of what Oedipus decides to do, he will kill his father and sleep with his mother. His choices make no difference as to whether these two events will happen.

This sort of fate is compatible either with determinism or a denial of determinism. Furthermore, with determinism one's choices really do affect the way the future will unfold. It is just that those choices couldn't have happened other than they do. Determinism is perhaps more and less restrictive than the sort of fate that operates in cases like that of Oedipus. If determinism is true; given the past, things couldn't have occurred other than they occurred. This includes every action we perform. But on determinism; if the past had gone differently, things in the future *could* go very differently. In Oedipus' case; whatever happens in the immediate past and present, Oedipus will kill his father and sleep with his mother. In his case, changing the immediate past and present won't change the future in these respects.

What happened about a hundred years ago to change views on the truth of determinism? It actually was a series of scientific discoveries concerning the behavior of very small objects (like atoms and parts of atoms). They appeared to behave in ways that imply that determinism is false. The branch of physics that focuses on the behavior of very small objects is called *quantum mechanics*. Physicists and philosophers tended to think that quantum mechanics implied that determinism is false (that is, that *indeterminism* is true). In particular, they thought that given the past and laws of nature, there are many possible futures. At best we can at best assign probabilities to the various possible futures.

Philosophers of physics (though perhaps not many physicists) now generally think that our observations of the behavior of very small objects and mathematical descriptions of those behaviors are consistent with determinism's being true. That means we return to a place we were before the early twentieth century, in that we can't tell by looking at the world scientifically whether determinism is true or not. For all of the experience you have of the world, it might be that everything you do is determined by the basic rules that govern the universe and the way the universe was long ago. Perhaps you're thinking, "Wait a minute. I make choices all the time! Surely determinism has to be false, then." But the truth of determinism doesn't preclude your making choices. Determinism simply implies that given the way the laws of nature are and the past was, you have to make the choices you make.

Maybe you're inclined to retort, "OK. But I'm certain I could have chosen other than I did. I could have not picked up this book a few minutes ago. I did pick it up, but I could have done other than I did." Not if determinism is true! And how would things appear to us if determinism were true? They'd appear exactly as they do now. We would think that there were various possible courses available to us. We would think that we could do other than we actually did.

It is natural to ask whether our acting freely and being responsible (I will assume here, not entirely uncontroversially, that these two concepts are equivalent) are consistent with determinism's being true. If everything I do is a function of the basic rules that govern the universe and the way the universe was long ago, could I still act freely? Philosophers who think that the truth of determinism precludes free will are known as *incompatibilists*. Philosophers who think that it is possible to act freely even if determinism is true are known as *compatibilists*.

Incompatibilists think that a necessary condition for my acting freely is that I could have done other than what I actually did. For instance, if I'm free with respect to typing this sentence, I could have refrained from typing it. Maybe you're thinking, "Sure, if you had spilled water into your keyboard and were cleaning it up, you wouldn't have typed the sentence. Or, if someone stole your computer earlier in the day, you wouldn't have typed the sentence." Both of these are, of course, true. But this isn't what the incompatibilist means when she says that free will requires the ability to do other than what I did. Rather, she means *in the exact circumstances in which I acted*, I could have done other than what I did. As things actually were before I typed that sentence, no one had stolen my computer; and there was no water on the keyboard. The incompatibilist asks: If we hold fixed the way things were until just before the decision, are there possible scenarios in which I don't type the sentence? If there aren't, I am not free, says the incompatibilist.

Compatibilists deny that in order to act freely I have to be able to have done other than what I actually did, in the above sense. What does free will consist in, then, for a compatibilist? Typically, compatibilists think that I act freely if an action is caused in an appropriate manner by my mental states. For instance, a view that many compatibilists have held is that I act freely with respect to typing a sentence if I want to type the sentence, and my wanting to type the sentence causes me to type the sentence. Clearly, my wanting to type the sentence can cause my typing the sentence even if determinism is true.

Now that we have some basic concepts that arise in debates around free will, we're going to engage in some philosophical reasoning using them. One of the most important thinkers around free will in the last fifty years is the American philosopher Peter van Inwagen. As a way of thinking more deeply about free will, I want to focus on two arguments he gives. The first is an argument that free will is not consistent with determinism. The second is an argument that free will is not consistent with indeterminism. (Question: If both of these are good arguments, what should be conclude about free will? We will answer this question a bit later.)

The first argument from van Inwagen we will consider is the **Consequence Argument**. The argument proceeds as follows. Assume (for the sake of the argument) that determinism is true. The first premise is that I have no control over the laws of nature and the total state of the universe long before I was born. The second premise is that I also have no control over the fact that the laws of nature and the total state of the universe imply that I will type this sentence now. Thus, van Inwagen concludes, I have no control over my typing this sentence now. That is to say, I am not free with respect to typing it. Of course, we could have picked any action to use in the argument. So, we conclude that if determinism is true, there is no free will.

We will evaluate the Consequence Argument in a bit. First, I want to state the second argument from van Inwagen, the **Rollback Argument**. Recall that the incompatibilist thinks that free will requires the ability to do otherwise. Let us assume I am free in this sense with respect to an action—say, taking a drink of coffee. Then, it was possible for me *in the exact same circumstances* in which I took the drink of coffee to refrain from drinking the coffee. Suppose that immediately after I take a drink of coffee, God (we're not actually committed to the existence of God for this argument, but it makes the argument slightly smoother to talk as though God does exist) stops the universe, rolls it back to just before the action, and lets it run forward again. Suppose further that God does this 10 trillion times. What would we observe? Presumably in some (perhaps the vast majority of) cases I take a drink of the coffee, and in others I don't. Why think this? Because I *can* do otherwise with respect to drinking the coffee. Presumably, then, if you run the scenario over enough times, sometimes I *will* do other than what I actually do. But notice what we're saying here: There is nothing different (apart from the decision itself) between the cases where I drink the coffee and those in which I don't. My desire for coffee or caffeine hasn't changed, my beliefs about the health effects of coffee haven't changed, my health hasn't changed, etc. Everything is *exactly* the same. Yet sometimes I drink the coffee, and others I don't. This makes it seem as though my drinking of the coffee is random and unconnected to any reasons I have to drink coffee; and surely no such random action can be free. Thus, it seems as though free will isn't consistent with indeterminism.

Earlier, I asked you what we should conclude if we took both the Consequence and Rollback arguments to be sound. If the Consequence Argument is sound, then free will is incompatible with determinism. If the Rollback Argument is sound, then free will is incompatible with indeterminism. But in any possible situation either determinism or indeterminism is true. Thus, free will is *impossible* if both these arguments are sound.

Thus, if we think we have free will, or *could* have free will, there must be something wrong with one or both of these arguments. Let's take a look at each, beginning with the Consequence Argument.

There are two sorts of ways philosophers (most of whom are compatibilists) have argued that the Consequence Argument is unsound. Both of these are ways of claiming the argument is *not valid*. (Recall from our first chapter what it is for an argument to be valid and sound.) Philosophers claim that it is possible that: (i) it is true that I have no control over the laws of nature and the total state of the universe in the distant past; and (ii) it is true I have no control over the fact that the laws and this distant state imply that I will take a drink of coffee; but (iii) it is *false* that I have no control over taking a drink of coffee. How could this be? How could (i) and (ii) be true while (iii) is false? One way to show this is to propose a particular analysis of having control over an action, and more generally having control over the truth of a proposition. This analysis, when used in the premises of the Consequence Argument, can be used to generate an invalidity, some argue. Suppose that one has control over performing an action if one would have performed it if one had chosen to perform it. Suppose further that one has control over the truth of a proposition if one would have made it true (or false) if one had chosen to make it true (or false). In this sense of having control, I don't have control over the distant past and laws of nature, and I don't have control over the fact that the distant past and laws of nature imply that I will take a drink of coffee. But I *do* have control over whether I will take a drink of coffee: If I had chosen to take a drink of coffee, I would have taken the drink of coffee. So on this interpretation of "having control," the Consequence Argument turns out to be invalid; it is possible for its premises to be true and conclusion false.

This analysis of what it is to have control fails, though. It is too permissive; there are cases where if I had chosen to perform an action

I would have performed it, even though I am not able to perform it (and thus don't have control over performing it). Suppose I had a bad experience with rum as a teenager. I drank far too much of it and wound up in the hospital with alcohol poisoning. I now cannot stand the smell of rum, or even the taste of rum-flavored candies and cakes. Indeed, I'm so affected by the experience that I'm not even able to choose to drink rum. Suppose someone puts a shot of rum in front of me and asks me to drink it. Do I have control over my drinking it? It seems I don't. I simply don't have the ability to drink it. Even thinking about drinking it makes me ill. But, on this analysis of having control, I *do* have control over my drinking it: If I had chosen to drink it, I would have drunk it. We may then conclude that this analysis of having control over an action is flawed.

Thus, this first way of claiming the Consequence Argument is invalid fails. There is a second tack the opponent of the Consequence Argument may take, however. This is the more common manner whereby one denies the validity of the argument. This is simply to deny that the form of inference in the Consequence Argument is a valid one. The argument is valid just if: If I don't have control over the truth of some claim p, and I don't have control over that p implies some other claim q; then (necessarily) I don't have a choice over the truth of q. But why think *that* is a valid inference form? Certainly, there are other forms of inference that are structurally similar and valid. But there are others that are structurally similar and invalid. The compatibilist who thinks she has strong support for her view may look at the Consequence Argument and insist that it must be invalid. For its premises are actually true (on the assumption of determinism) and its conclusion false.

The question arises, then, as to who has the burden of proof in the debate over the validity of the main form of inference in the Consequence Argument. It seems to me that the compatibilist is within her rights in expecting the defender of the argument to provide some reason for thinking the Consequence Argument is valid. It's worth noting that the analysis of control over an action that we just examined actually *gives a reason* for thinking the inference in the argument is invalid. So if that analysis of control had worked, the opponent of the Consequence Argument would be in a stronger position to deny its validity.

Suppose you're in a position of finding the inference from premises to conclusion in the Consequence Argument to be a valid one. You then will want to know if there are reasons to reject the argument's premises. Objections to the premises of the Consequence Argument have focused on its first premise: I have no control over the total state of the universe in the distant past together with the laws of nature. The important contemporary American philosopher David Lewis has argued that I could make it that something that is a law of nature wasn't a law of nature. (This is not the same as actually breaking a law of nature, which we cannot do.) Others have argued that I could act in a way such that the past was different. (This is not the same as causing the past to be different than it is, which we cannot do.) If I could act so that something that was a law of nature wasn't, or such that the past were different from the way it is; it would seem that the first premise of the Consequence Argument is in trouble.

The philosophical details get very complex at this point. I will simply note that it seems to me that one is able to show that the first premise of the Consequence Argument is false via the non-fixity of the past or laws of nature only if one assumes first that compatibilism is true. If this is true, the defender of the Consequence Argument need not worry. Why? Because one has a reply to the first premise of the argument only if one antecedently assumes that the overall main conclusion of the argument is false! But this is a debate in which currently much philosophical work and progress is occurring, and it remains to be seen how the dust will settle after this work and progress.

The other argument from Peter van Inwagen we stated was the Rollback Argument. What have incompatibilists had to say about it? First, it seems that the incompatibilist must accept the facts of the case as they're stated in the argument. If God many times were to roll back the universe to immediately before my incompatibilist-free decision about drinking the coffee and were to let things unfold from there, it is clear what would happen: Sometimes I would drink the coffee and sometimes I wouldn't. This is just what it means for my decision to be undetermined. Then, to reply to the Rollback Argument, what the incompatibilist must do is tell a particular sort of story. According to this story, the facts of the case in the Rollback Argument don't imply that my drinking coffee is random in a way that precludes it from being free. To see how the incompatibilist might do this, suppose I have a very minor seizure that causes my arm to shoot out from my body. Suppose further the connection between the seizure and the movement of the arm isn't deterministic; that is, suppose I could have the seizure (and everything else stay the same) and my arm not shoot out. No one would want to argue that my arm's shooting out was a free action, even though it wasn't determined.

Now, imagine a case where I decide to stick my arm out and then it sticks out. But it was consistent with the total state of the universe right before the action that I not stick my arm out. What is different between this case where my action isn't determined and the seizure case where my action isn't determined? One seemingly-important difference lies in the cause of my arm's movement. In the first case, it is the seizure that causes my arm to move. In the second case, *I* cause my arm to move. What sort of thing am I? In this context, we can say I am an *agent*, the sort of thing who is capable of acting for reasons.

Some philosophers have thought that there is a particular sort of causation, *agent causation,* which is fundamentally different from the sort of causation one has when a baseball breaks a window or a nail punctures a tire. This is the view taken by the eighteenth-century Scottish philosopher Thomas Reid, and more recently by the twentieth century American philosopher Roderick Chisholm. Each thinks that agent causation is a unique sort of causation, and that the fact that an action is agent-caused in the right sort of manner makes it non-random (even while undetermined). So long as I—an agent—cause my drinking coffee, then it isn't random in a way that would make it unfree. Thus, we have a reply to the Rollback Argument.

What should we think of this reply to the Rollback Argument? There does seem to be a real difference between the case of the seizure causing my arm to move; and the case where I for particular reasons cause my arm to move. But how does this difference in the source of the action ameliorate the concern that the action is random? We don't have an account of how adding the agent is supposed to help with the randomness. Why can't the defender of the Rollback Argument insist that, even with the agent, there still is randomness that precludes freedom?

Above we mentioned acting for reasons, and I think that we might make progress in our reply to the Rollback Argument if we appeal to this concept. Let's compare my arm's shooting out as a result of the seizure; with my arm's moving because I decided, for various reasons, to move it. The latter does involve an agent, me. But it is in the context of an event: my having various reasons to move my arm. Let's put these scenarios explicitly.

Event A: My having a seizure
Event B: My arm's moving
Event C: My having various reasons for moving my arm.

Case 1: Event A causes Event B.
Case 2: Event C causes Event B.

Each of A–C are events. Thus, we need not appeal to any unique sort of causation here, as we did with agent causation. If you were to ask me why my arm moved in the non-seizure case, I could reply: It moved because of reasons I had (I was trying to stretch my arm, or the like).

Perhaps you're thinking: "But can't we run the rollback scenario with the agent or person acting for reasons? It still will be the case that if God rolls back the universe, sometimes you will drink the coffee, and sometimes you won't. This holds even if we construe the event causing the coffee drinking as your having coffee-drinking reasons." There is a clear answer to this: Yes, we absolutely can run the rollback scenario with this new explanation of the cause of my coffee drinking. But notice how far we are from something that is truly random, like a seizure, causing the action. Now we have a subject's having reasons causing the action. The reasons explain why the action occurs, rather than any other action. To say that in the rollback scenarios sometimes I drink coffee and others I don't is just to note that the coffee drinking isn't determined. It isn't to say that it is random. And if you change the reasons in the causing event, you will change the probabilities that a particular action will occur.

In this chapter, we've thought philosophically about the nature of free will. We began by looking at two different views about the compatibility of free will and determinism—compatibilism and incompatibilism. We then looked at two arguments given by Peter van Inwagen—the Consequence Argument and Rollback Argument. We left room for the compatibilist to reject the Consequence Argument, either by rejecting its validity or by denying its first premise is true. We then gave an account on which the incompatibilist may reject the claim implicit in the Rollback Argument that free will requires determinism.

Reflection Questions

1 What is determinism? Indeterminism?

2 What is quantum mechanics? What relation is it thought to have to determinism?

3 What is compatibilism? Incompatibilism?

4 What is the Consequence Argument? What might the compatibilist say about it?

5 What is the Rollback Argument? What might the incompatibilist say about it?

FURTHER READING

The last forty years have seen a great deal of groundbreaking philosophical work on the nature of free will. Much of the work is highly technical. One excellent and fairly-accessible book is *A Contemporary Introduction to Free Will* (Oxford, 2005) by Robert Kane. Gary Watson has collected many important papers in free will in his anthology *Free Will* (Oxford, 2003). In this volume is a statement from Peter van Inwagen of the Consequence Argument, Roderick Chisholm's paper in which he defends agent causation, and the paper in which David Lewis argues that the first premise of the Consequence Argument is false. Daniel Speak's entry on the Consequence Argument in *The Oxford Companion to Free will* (2011) provides a nice overview of the argument. Van Inwagen gives the Rollback Argument in "Free will Remains a Mystery" in his *Thinking About Free Will* (Cambridge, 2017). Laura Ekstrom pushes back on van Inwagen's overall argument about free will being a mystery in "Free will is Not a Mystery" *the Oxford Companion to Free will (2011)*. Tim Maudlin discusses the connection between quantum mechanics and determinism in his *Quantum Non-Locality and Relativity: Metaphysical Intimations of Modern Physics.* (Wiley-Blackwell, 2011). The view at the end of the chapter in which an event consisting of a person's having reasons is what causes actions my own view that I developed in the late 1990s, though I've not published it. The idea of framing a discussion about free will around the Consequence Argument and Rollback Argument came from a talk John Fischer gave in 2010.

Question 5

WHAT IS GOD LIKE?

More than half of the world's population are monotheists of some sort. Monotheists believe that there exists a very powerful being—God—that created the world, and this being is substantially more powerful than any other being. The vast majority of monotheists are adherents of the Abrahamic religions: Jews, Christians, and Muslims. Also, the vast majority of monotheists think that God is all-powerful ("omnipotent"), all-knowing ("omniscient"), and perfectly good. In this chapter, we are going to reflect both on the nature of God, and how monotheists think we have rational beliefs about the nature of God.

I. Knowledge of God's Nature

According to monotheists, how is it that we come to have well-founded beliefs about what God is like? Typically, for monotheists there are two principal sources of these beliefs. The first is from important religious texts, such as the Hebrew Bible, New Testament, Quran, Avesta, and parts of Hindu scriptures like the Upanishads and Bhagavad Gita. Monotheists believe these sorts of texts are, in some sense, given to us by God. And they believe they give us a picture of what God is like. We can call these sorts of sources *revealed theology*. From revealed theology we learn at least that God is very powerful, knows a great deal, and is good.

The second source of rational belief about God is from *pure reason*. We may start with features of God we get from revealed theology, and reason our way to a deeper understanding of the nature of God. The principal manner of acquiring rational belief about the nature of God from pure reason is known as "perfect-being theology." It has its roots in the work of the great medieval philosopher and theologian, Anselm of Canterbury. Perfect-being theology starts from the claim (which we may draw from revealed theology) that God is maximally great—the greatest possible being. We then deduce, using reason alone, other attributes of God. (Anselm even thought that he could deduce the *existence* of God using perfect-being theology.) For instance, we can ask ourselves: If God is the greatest possible being, how powerful must God be? We might then conclude God must be omnipotent or maximally powerful if God is the greatest possible being. Why think this? Suppose that God were only somewhat-powerful. Then we could imagine a greater being, one just like God but that was more powerful. But then God wouldn't be the greatest possible being. So God must be omnipotent. We arrive at this using pure reason, having started with the proposition that God is the greatest possible being.

Monotheists come to have well-founded beliefs about God typically from a mix of both revealed theology and pure reason. Of course, different sorts of monotheists have different beliefs about the nature of God. For instance, Christians typically believe in the Trinity—that God is comprised of three persons. Muslims and Jews deny that God exists in three persons. But there is a core conception of God that all monotheists typically hold. This conception is that God is the greatest possible being, and is *omnicompetent*: omniscient, omnipotent, and perfectly good. That God is omnicompetent is almost certainly a doctrine that comes both from revealed theology and pure reason. (What we see in holy religious texts are claims along the lines that God is very powerful and knows a great deal.) In the rest of this chapter, we are going to examine the implications of God's being both the greatest possible being and omnicompetent. What sort of being is a being who is maximally great, omniscient, omnipotent, and perfectly good?

II. God, Time, and Existence

Monotheists deny that God ever came into being at a time in the past. In this way, God is fundamentally different than something like a car, the earth, or the solar system. This claim is consistent with two different views about the relation between God and time. On the first view, God is an everlasting, temporal being. God always has existed, and always will exist. But God is "inside time" in that he experiences the passage of time. On the second view, God is atemporal. God is "outside of time", and as such doesn't experience the passage of time.

We will follow common convention and say that if God is everlasting but temporal, he is *sempiternal*. And if God is outside of time, he is *eternal*.

Why might someone favor one view over the other? A common concern is that if God is a temporal being he is subject to change. As time passes, God changes. And God isn't supposed to change. So God must be eternal.

But it's not at all clear that this is what people mean when they say God doesn't change. When theists claim that God is unchanging, typically they mean that God's character and general intentions don't change. God doesn't change his mind capriciously. God doesn't one day tell us to help certain people because they are poor, and the next to exploit the same people because they are poor. But one can hold to the view that God's central character doesn't change, while holding that God does undergo change. For instance, God believes that it is cloudy right now in Southern California. Later he will believe that it is sunny in Southern California. This is a real change, though not the sort of change most theists would be concerned about.

Some people think that if God were a temporal being, we couldn't act freely. If God foreknew that I would type this sentence, then I can't do other than to type it. And that entails that I don't type it freely. But I do type it freely, so God must be eternal. (This is famously the reasoning of the sixth-century philosopher and theologian Boethius.) Thus, there seems to be a problem between divine foreknowledge and human free will that seemingly is avoided if God is eternal. An atemporal being doesn't have past, present, or future knowledge.

One immediate concern many have had with this attempted solution to problems of the compatibility of divine foreknowledge and human free will is that a very similar problem arises with God's atemporal, eternal knowledge. If God eternally knows that I will type this sentence, then I can't help but type it. And thus I'm not free with respect to typing the sentence. We will return to the argument that divine foreknowledge is incompatible with human free will in the next section.

One worry for the person who thinks that God is eternal is that God seems to react to events in time. For instance, theists believe God gets angry when humans do bad things. Sometimes he will react to these actions by smiting the offending humans. It's not at all clear this sort of reaction is coherent if God is outside of time. To the extent that God is reacting to events that occur in time, it strongly suggests that God is a temporal being.

III. Omnipotence

Monotheists also think that God is omnipotent, or all powerful. Spelling out what this means is tricky, though. Here's a first shot: To be omnipotent is to be able to do anything at all, possible or impossible. Thus, if God is omnipotent, she can make a plane figure that is both a triangle and a circle. She can make a married bachelor. And so on. But theists (the great medieval philosopher and theologian St. Thomas Aquinas is a good example of this) have tended to avoid this conception of omnipotence for fear of lapsing into incoherence. What does it mean to say that God can do impossible things? Presumably if God can do some impossible things, she can do any impossible thing. Does that mean that God can make it such that she both does and doesn't exist? But that doesn't make any sense!

Then, maybe we should say that God can do anything that is *possible*. But this faces problems, as well. Here is one thing that is possible (I've done it!): endure hours of physical therapy after tearing ligaments in one's ankle. But God can't do that. Here's another one: take aspirin after waking up with a hangover. God can't do that, either.

Maybe the problem is that these sorts of events involve bodies, and God doesn't have a body. Then, maybe we should say that God can do anything that is possible for something without a body to do. But this won't work, either. A poltergeist lacks a body, and spends its time causing mischief and intentionally scaring human beings. Presumably God can't do that, either.

Maybe, then, we should say that to be omnipotent is to be able to do anything that God is able to do. Suppose, though, that God could do only very little. Then, on this definition, one could be substantially less powerful than God actually is and still be omnipotent.

Saying what it is for a being to be omnipotent, at least if we're trying to do so in terms of abilities, is difficult. (I think it probably can be done, though; and at the end of the chapter I refer the reader to a fairly sophisticated attempt to do this.) Is there another way to say what it is for God to be omnipotent? Maybe we can say that for God to be omnipotent is for God to be maximally powerful—to be such that no other possible being could have more power. You might notice that this doesn't really tell us what omnipotence *is* in the way the other attempted definitions do. The upside of this is that it isn't subject to the sorts of counterexamples our other conceptions of omnipotence are.

Sometimes in discussions of omnipotence one encounters "the paradox of the stone." It is a very old puzzle, and it goes like this: Can

God create a stone so heavy she can't lift it? If she can, then there is something she can't do (lift the stone); and thus she isn't omnipotent. If she can't, then there is something she can't do (create the stone); and thus she isn't omnipotent. Thus, God isn't omnipotent.

This is clearly a valid argument, so what should the theist say about its premises? The standard reply to the paradox of the stone is to point out that there being a stone so heavy God can't lift it is not a possible state of affairs. If one requires that God only be able to bring about possible states of affairs, then God's ability to bring this about doesn't affect her omnipotence. (And if God can bring about the impossible, then she can bring it about that she can lift a stone that she can't lift!) But a worry here is that there are other ways of describing the events here that don't seem to involve impossibilities. For instance, here is another way of describing the stone event: There being a stone so heavy that the individual trying to lift it can't lift it. Here is another way: There being a stone so heavy that its creator can't lift it. Both of these seem to be possible, so it appears we aren't able to avoid the paradox of the stone here as easily as we did at first.

IV. Omniscience

In contrast to omnipotence, omniscience is fairly straightforward to characterize. To be omniscient is to know all true propositions. (We don't need to worry about false propositions, as they can't be known.) Where philosophers disagree is over which true propositions there are. The sort of propositions most discussed in this regard are propositions about the future free actions of creatures. For instance, consider the proposition *In five minutes I will take a drink of coffee*. Some philosophers think that this is a true proposition, and that as a result God knows it. Others think that if this proposition were true and God knew it, that I wouldn't be free with respect to drinking my coffee. The argument for this is straightforward. If God knows *that in five minutes I will take a drink of coffee*, then I will take a drink of coffee. (Again, only true propositions can be known.) If I will take a drink of coffee, it's not possible for me not to take a drink of coffee. But then I am not free with respect to taking a drink of coffee.

In response to this sort of argument, some philosophers deny there are any true propositions about the future free actions of creatures. They typically will deny that they adopt this view just to avoid problems with free will. Rather, they will say that prior to a free creature's acting, there is nothing to be known about whether the creature will perform a particular action. When the creature performs the action, then God knows it *is* performing the action. After the creature performs the action, God knows it *did* perform the action. But there is nothing to be known about whether the creature *will* perform the action, beyond the probability that one will perform the action.

Thus, these philosophers deny God has foreknowledge of the future free actions of creatures. God doesn't know if I will take a drink of coffee in five minutes, or not. How does God make things work out the way he wants if he doesn't foreknow what we will do? He does the best he can knowing what we are *likely* to do. God knows that it is very unlikely that in five minutes I will drink a piña colada. He knows it is pretty likely I will drink some coffee. But either of these actions is consistent with what God knows now. Philosophers who deny that God knows the future free actions of creatures are called *open theists* (so-called because they believe the future is robustly open). Open theism has been met with significant criticism from many traditional theists, who see it as undermining the sovereignty of God.

Let's return to our argument that if God foreknows what I will do, I am not free. Suppose I am concerned that a God without foreknowledge of human free actions leaves too much to chance in terms of his governance of the world. Are there ways to reply to the argument for the incompatibility of foreknowledge and free will other than with open theism?

It turns out there are. One way is to deny that free will requires the ability to do other than what I do. As we discussed in the last chapter, this view is known as *compatibilism*. A second way is to claim that the past is not fixed in the way we might have thought that it is fixed. Consider two claims that are about the past.

a) World War II occurred after World War I.
b) God knew 1,000,000 years ago that I would drink coffee in five minutes from now.

Typically, we want to say that there is nothing I can do about the past. Suppose I spilled some milk a few minutes ago. I may regret doing this, and I may try to avoid doing so in the future. But there is nothing I can do *now* to change the fact that it occurred. It is in the past and thus is fixed. Similarly, that World War II occurred after World War I also is fixed. There's nothing anyone can do now to change the truth of that proposition.

However, consider (b), above. It also is about the past, in some sense: It describes how things were 1,000,000 years ago. But there seems to be something I *can* do about the truth of (b). What's that? Well, I can refrain from drinking the coffee! Thus, the truth of (b) seems to be up to me in a way the truth of (a) is not. Perhaps, then, the past is not altogether fixed in the way we might have thought.

How does this help with the argument that divine foreknowledge precludes human free will? Suppose God knows that in five minutes I will drink coffee. Then I will drink coffee, of course. But does this mean that I can't do otherwise with respect to drinking the coffee? No, some philosophers say. I can refrain from drinking the coffee. But wouldn't that imply that God was wrong about the future? No, these philosophers say. Had I refrained from drinking the coffee, God would have known all along that I wasn't going to drink the coffee.

Philosophers who think that we have this sort of power over the past are known as *Ockhamists*. (The view was first stated by William of Ockham, a fourteenth century English philosopher and theologian. If the name sounds familiar, you may have heard of "Ockham's Razor," the claim that one shouldn't posit more entities than are necessary to account for some phenomenon one is trying to explain.) We should be clear about what the Ockhamists believe and don't believe. Ockhamists don't think that I can cause the past to be different than it is. I can't cause the spilled milk not to have been spilled, or change where I went to university. But, there are some facts that are true in the past, but that make reference to the present moment (like (b), above); and those I *do* have power over. Those sorts of facts are the ones that cause the problem for free will from divine foreknowledge.

As you might imagine, there have been significant disputes over Ockhamism. I will note one concern here. Consider the concrete belief state God had 1,000,000 ago that is involved with the belief that in five minutes I will drink coffee. If I refrain from drinking the coffee, then that seems to change. But isn't that saying I have the power to change the past in some objectionable way? Isn't that like saying that I have the ability to change where I went to university?

V. Perfect Goodness

Monotheists also believe that God is perfectly good. It is worth noting that there is *prima facie* (Latin for "on the face of it") contradictory evidence concerning the goodness of God from religious texts. God is described as good throughout scriptures like the Hebrew Bible, New Testament, and Quran. But God is also depicted as engaging in some evil behavior in places like the Hebrew Bible (e.g., ordering a genocide, or mauling children with bears after they mocked a prophet for being bald). Thus, a theist needs to square various data (from both revealed and perfect-being theology) about the goodness of God. Typically, this will involve denying that God engaged in the behavior in question, or that, appearances to the contrary notwithstanding, it was morally fine for God to do what she did. Theists typically take the perfect goodness of God as a nonnegotiable, so we will examine perfect goodness as an attribute of God. (It is worth noting that not all theists reach this conclusion. Marcion, a second-century Christian, thought that the principal divine being depicted in the Hebrew Bible was so different morally from the principal divine being in the New Testament that they must be two different beings!)

Here is a concern that might occur to you if you think for a bit about perfect goodness. If God is perfectly good, how can she be free? Perfect goodness involves making things as good as one can make them. But that means that God can't do anything but make things that way. But that means that God isn't free; she has to do what she does, as dictated by her perfect goodness. How can it be that God isn't free?

There are a couple things the theist might say in reply to this argument. First, the argument assumes that it's not possible that God not be perfectly good. But maybe God could do something less than the very best; and if she did, God would simply not then be perfectly good.

Suppose though that this isn't an option for the theist. What then might she say in reply to the argument against divine freedom from divine goodness? One thing she might question is whether there *is* a best way things could be. Maybe for each way things could be, there is some way better than it. How would God decide how to make things, then? Presumably there would be some amount of goodness that God would have to make actual. But above that level, God is able to choose from any scenario she wanted. So, many possible scenarios wouldn't be good enough. But many would be good enough, and God could choose any of those.

There is something else the theist could say. She could accept compatibilism about divine free will and deny that God's being unable to create anything but the best world implies that God is unfree. God is able to do exactly as she wants, and there is no impediment to her acting on her desires. She wants to make the best possible world, and she does that, and she thus acts freely. (This is the line taken by Gottfried Leibniz.)

Reflection Questions

1 What is the paradox of the stone?

2 Why might someone think that divine foreknowledge of actions is inconsistent with their being free?

3 What is open theism? How is it a solution to problems of divine foreknowledge and freewill?

4 What is Ockhamism? How is it a solution to problems of divine foreknowledge and freewill?

5 Which solution to the problem of divine foreknowledge and human free will do you find most plausible?

6 Why might someone think that God's being perfectly good is a problem for divine free will? What might someone say in reply to this problem?

FURTHER READING

I recommend highly the recent book *The Philosophy of Religion* (Blackwell, 2016) by Edward Wierenga. It contains extended discussion of all the issues in this chapter, including a sophisticated discussion of ability definitions of omnipotence. You will note that the line I take on the standard reply to the paradox of the stone hews close to that of Wierenga's. Another good book on the nature of God is Eleonore Stump's *The God of the Bible and the God of the Philosophers* (Marquette, 2016). The text that served as a manifesto for contemporary open theism is *The Openness of God* (IVP 1994). A sophisticated analysis of the problem of foreknowledge and free will can be found in Linda Zagzebski's *The Dilemma of Freedom and Foreknowledge* (Oxford, 1991).

Question 6

WHAT IS TIME?

All of us think about and talk about time frequently (indeed; all the time!). We wonder what time it is. We try to determine if we have enough time to do what we want to do. We notice that time appears to pass more quickly as we age. And so on. But what exactly *is* time? This is a difficult question to answer. (Indeed, getting clear on what would count as a thoroughly adequate answer to this question is itself difficult.) We're going to try to begin to answer this general question about the nature of time by considering answers to several more particular questions about time.

Question 1: Is time real?

You may think the answer to Question 1 is obvious: Of course, it is real. We think about it many times a day. Processes and events unfold in time. Indeed, one of the clearest facts there is is that time exists. But some philosophers, such as the ancient Greek philosopher Parmenides and the early twentieth-century philosopher J.M.E. McTaggart, have denied that time exists. Philosophers who deny that time exists typically think that reality consists of a single, unchanging object— what we will call the Universe. What is the Universe? We might be tempted to say that it is the massive object that has every other material object as parts. But that wouldn't be right; for if the massive object has parts, then more than one thing exists (the thing and each of its parts). Then, maybe we might say it is the massive thing that *appears* to have every other material object as parts: If there were things like chairs and tables and planets and dogs, it would have them as parts. Parmenides thought that the appearance that there are many distinct objects and that they change over time are illusions. All that exists is the Universe, says Parmenides.

I think we should deny that it is an illusion both that there are distinct objects, and that they change over time. It is philosophically fruitful to consider arguments that reality consists in a single, unchanging thing; or that otherwise we should think that there is no such thing as time. (See the end of the chapter for further reading on this.) But surely there is such a thing as time, and thus surely any argument that has as a conclusion that time doesn't exist must be unsound.

Question 2: Are past and future times as real as the present time?

Suppose, then, *pace* (Latin for "contrary to") Parmenides, time does exist. One thing that we typically say exists in time are events. The

event of my pressing these keys is present. The event of World War II
is past. The event of the celebrating the coming of the year 3000 is
future. This much seems straightforward. But do the non-present
events (the second and third) *exist*? Recall our list we made in
discussing technological immortality in chapter 3. Suppose, like we
did there, that we made a list of everything there is, full stop; would it
include wholly past and future events? More generally, would it
include any wholly future or wholly past objects or entities?

On one view of the nature of time, the answer is "no; only present
things exist." This view is called *presentism*. The presentist thinks
that there are no wholly past or future objects or events; only the
present is real.

On another view of the nature of time—*eternalism*—the answer is
"yes." The eternalist thinks that past and future objects and events are
as real as present objects and events. For instance, according to the
eternalist, World War II exists. If we were to list everything that exists,
on the list would be World War II. It's not present—simultaneous with
my writing of this sentence—of course. But it does exist. The same goes
for my great grandmother. She exists, too. She doesn't exist at present—
simultaneous with my writing of this sentence—but she does exist.

The eternalist thinks that time is similar to space in this regard. As
I type this sentence in California, I can note that Australia exists. It
doesn't exist *here*—where I type this sentence—but it does exist. The
eternalist will say the same thing about World War II: It doesn't exist
now, but it does exist. We commonsensically think that all places are
equally real; there is nothing metaphysically special about the present
place where I am. The same goes for time, says the eternalist. There is
nothing metaphysically special about the present time, either.

The eternalist typically will talk about an amalgam of time and space called *spacetime*. Spacetime is a four-dimensional object consisting of three spatial dimensions and one temporal dimension. It can be difficult for us to imagine what four-dimensional spacetime is, but we can try to do so using three-dimensional objects. To do this, we suppress one of the three spatial dimensions and let it represent time. Consider a long baguette. We can model spacetime by letting the length of the baguette represent the temporal dimension of spacetime, and the width and height of the baguette represent two of the three spatial dimensions of spacetime. Call one end of the baguette "A", and the other end of the baguette "B." Parts of the baguette close to A are just as real as parts close to B. Similarly, the corresponding parts of spacetime are equally real. Our baguette representation of spacetime conveys the eternalist notion that all regions of spacetime are equally real. (We will return to our baguette momentarily.)

On a third view of the nature of time—*the growing block view*—the past and present are equally real, though the future is not. It is a sort of mid-way view between presentism and eternalism. This view was championed by the philosopher C.D. Broad in the first half of the twentieth century. The growing block view has some initial intuitive plausibility: On it, the already-happened past exists, though the not-yet-happened future doesn't.

One's view of time has implications for one's view of the nature of material objects. A presentist typically thinks that material objects are three dimensional and are wholly present at each time they exist. The whole of my computer existed a second ago, and the whole of it exists now. It persists through time and change by being wholly present at different times. An eternalist or growing block theorist typically thinks that objects are spread out in time as well as in space. Thus, objects are four dimensional. Return to our very long baguette. Recall that the length of the baguette represents the temporal dimension of spacetime, and the height and width represent two of the three spatial dimensions of spacetime. We can represent objects in spacetime by sticking pencils into the baguette length-wise. Let the pencil represent any ordinary object, say the table at which I am sitting. The pencil is spread out in three dimensions in the baguette—two spatial dimensions and one temporal dimension. This is to say that the pencil represents an object (a table) with both spatial and temporal parts. Eternalists and growing block theorists typically say that ordinary objects (like this table) have both spatial and temporal parts.

We can better understand temporal parts by thinking about events. Consider a football match. A match (typically) consists of two parts, each of which last forty-five minutes. These parts are temporal parts. In addition, the match will occur in particular regions of space (a particular stadium like Anfield, say).

On what basis might someone choose between different views about the metaphysical status of past and future times and objects? Here are a few considerations that philosophers will point to in deciding between different views.

Consideration 1: Cross-time causal relations.

Events in the past cause events in the present, and events in the present cause events in the future. If something causes something else or is an effect of something else, it must exist. Thus, the past and future exist. This tells in favor of eternalism.

With Consideration 1, we note the obvious fact that things in the past change the way things are now. For instance, we may say that the earthquake an hour ago caused my power to be off now. Then, we are saying that the earthquake stands in a causal relation to my power's being off now. But if things stand in relations to one another, each must exist. Thus, the past must exist. Similarly, my pressing the key now causes a letter to appear on my screen in the future. So, the future must exist, too.

Consideration 2: Thank goodness that's over.

Consideration 2 comes from the important twentieth century logician and philosopher Arthur Prior. Prior noted that when looking back on a painful experience that we sometimes will think that we're grateful that the experience is over and done with. When we say this, we're saying that it doesn't exist or isn't real anymore. But "on eternalism and the growing block view as we're construing it", it *does* exist. It's just not present. This tells in favor of presentism.

Consideration 3: From relativity.

This third argument has been defended by many people. Perhaps its best-known defense is from the important twentieth century American philosopher Hilary Putnam. According to Einstein's special theory of relativity, there can be an event E that lies in my future and your present, even though you are in my present. This effect is seen most clearly when you and I are moving very rapidly relative to one another. The presentist says that E exists if and only if E is present. But it is present for you, and not present for me. Does E exist then, or not? It appears that the presentist must say that it exists for you, but not for me—thus making existence relative to individuals, which is implausible. This tells in favor of eternalism.

Consideration 4: Things change.

Objects undergo change all the time. My wall was white, and now it is blue. What this means is that the *same object* was white, and now is blue. But only the presentist can say this. The non-presentists have to say that a past temporal part of the wall is white, and present temporal parts of the wall are blue. But it's false on these views that the *same thing* was white and now is blue. This tells in favor of presentism.

Different philosophers have given various sorts of replies to these Considerations. (See the end of the chapter for further references.) Some presentists have said, in reply to Consideration 1, that events are abstract objects that always exist. They *occur* typically for discrete durations of time, but they always exist. So the event of the earthquake does exist now (though isn't occurring now), and thus can stand in causal relations to my power's being out. Non-presentists have said in reply to the thank-goodness-that's-over objection that we celebrate something's being past in a way analogous to the way we are grateful that something bad happens far from us and not to us directly here. In reply to the objection from relativity, presentists have suggested that there is some absolute present according to which everything that is present relative to it exists, and that what exists isn't relative to individuals. And non-presentists have defended an account of change that involves different temporal parts having different properties.

I myself find Arthur Prior's thank-goodness-that's-over argument compelling. This inclines me to presentism over eternalism and the growing block view. But for me the strongest consideration in deciding between these three views will appear in answering the next question: Does time really pass?

Question 3: Does time *really* pass?

That time passes is an element of commonsense metaphysics. Yet, when given more careful scrutiny it can seem mysterious. What sort of thing *is* temporal passage? Relatedly, think of other sorts of passage; say, a driving trip across France. This passage occurs at a rate—say 300 km/day. What about the passage of time? Does it occur at a rate? It might seem that it couldn't. For, what is a rate? It is defined as a unit of distance over a unit of time. If time passes at a rate, we presumably then will understand this as involving a unit of temporal distance (seconds, minutes, etc.) over some time. This has to be a second time, though—a *hypertime*—in which time passes. (Time can't pass at a rate involving itself. It's unclear what that would even mean.) However, we then will ask about the *hypertime's* passage: At what rate does the hypertime pass? This presumably will be understood in terms of a hyper-hypertime, and suddenly we've a regress of hypertimes. But that's no good.

Maybe we then should say that temporal passage isn't like other sorts of passages. We call it "passage" but we shouldn't think that we are giving the sober metaphysical truth of the matter with this description. That is, it's not *actually* a passage, where a passage is something that occurs over a distance in a particular time. Rather, it is a *sui generis* (unique) sort of change—the becoming present of events that were future. Furthermore, temporal passage is not the sort of thing that occurs at a rate. We may talk about time going quickly or slowly (hopefully not the latter as you read this). But that sort of talk is loose and not designed to tell us the way reality actually is. This view of temporal passage is close to that of the mid-twentieth century British philosopher C.D. Broad.

Suppose Broad's view about the nature of temporal passage is correct. Earlier we looked at three views in the philosophy of time. What does each of them have to say about temporal passage? The first thing we can note is that for an eternalist, in some sense time *doesn't* pass. (The view is sometimes called the "static" view of time.) The eternalist will insist that there is also a sense in which it passes: Objects have different temporal parts at different times, and we can talk about time's passing in terms of these differing temporal parts. But the eternalist has nothing like the constant of the future's becoming present we have expressed in Broad's view of temporal passage. By contrast, both the presentist and the growing block theorist can allow for real passage of time. On each of these views, there is a metaphysical difference between future and present, and the future's becoming present involves some sort of robust change in reality.

Perhaps you're thinking that it is obvious that time passes in some robust manner, and that it doesn't on eternalism is a mark against eternalism. *I* think that this is right. But the eternalist has tried various ways to soften the blow of this problem. Usually the eternalist will claim that the feeling of temporal passage we have is something that we project onto the world, in the way that some people think that we project color onto the world (more on color and perception in chapter 9). Some people have tried to explain the origin our feeling of temporal passage by pointing to one-way phenomena we observe in nature (cause and effect goes from past to future, and entropy increases from past to future). But the lack of real temporal passage has bothered many eternalists (Einstein, for instance); and accounting for it is still a real problem for those who think there is no metaphysical difference between the future and present.

Question 4: Is time essentially related to change?

In the seventeenth century there were many debates between two of the most important thinkers of the last 500 years: Isaac Newton and Gottfried Leibniz. Perhaps the most famous debate between them was over who invented calculus. But there were others. One debate was over the nature of space. Newton thought that space could exist with nothing in it; space was a sort of container that held things. Leibniz thought that space couldn't exist without objects in it. For Leibniz, space isn't itself a separate thing, but is somehow parasitic on the relations that hold between objects in space. Newton's view is known as *absolutism* about space, and Leibniz's *relationalism* about space. Newton and Leibniz held views on time analogous to their views on space. Newton was an absolutist about time; he thought that time could exist without any change. Time exists independently of the behavior of any objects in time. Leibniz was a relationalist about time. He thought that time couldn't exist without change. Just as space is dependent on relations between objects in space, time is dependent on the changing of objects in time.

Why might someone favor absolutism about time over relationalism about time, or vice versa? To appreciate one reason, recall our discussion of thought experiments from the first chapter of this book. There we noted that thought experiments serve as an important source of evidence in philosophy. Then, here's a thought experiment you can try yourself: Image that the entire universe freezes for ten minutes, and during that time there is no change. At the end of this period, things resume changing as normal. The relationalist about time claims this scenario that I just described is impossible. If change stopped, time would stop, too. The absolutist about time claims this scenario is possible.

Leibniz himself thinks that if time were absolute that there would be no reason for God to create the world at one time rather than another. But this would violate the Principle of Sufficient Reason, that for any truth there is a sufficient reason why it is true. (Most philosophers reject the Principle of Sufficient Reason.)

At the end of the day, I find the argument that it is possible there be a universe in which everything stops moving for a duration of time compelling. So I reject that time must involve change.

Taking Stock

We began this chapter asking the question, "What is time?" As a means of trying to answer this question, we looked at answers to several more particular questions about time. What should we think about the various views we surveyed? I can tell you my own assessment of the terrain; your own philosophical intuitions may differ from mine. First, I think that time exists and absolutely does pass, so I reject both a view like Parmenides' and eternalism. I also find the thank-goodness-that's-over argument compelling, which inclines me toward presentism over the growing block view. And I think that there can be time without change. But none of the arguments here strike me as *obviously* sound, and really capable philosophers hold different views on all of these issues. Know that wherever you're inclined to land on the spectrum of views, you are in distinguished company.

Reflection Questions

1   What does Parmenides think about time?

2   What is presentism? Why might someone accept it?

3   What is eternalism? Why might someone accept it?

4   What is the growing block view? Why might someone accept it?

5   What are absolutism and relationalism about time? Why might someone choose one over the other?

6   Which view or views about the nature of time do you find most plausible? Why?

FURTHER READING

Save fragments of a poem ("On Nature"), we have almost nothing that survives from Parmenides. Much of what we think we know of him comes from other people writing about him, as Plato did in his dialogue *Parmenides* (which I recommend highly as a piece of literature and philosophy). Both some of "On Nature" and Plato's dialogue *Parmenides* can be found in *Plato and Parmenides* by Frances MacDonald Cornford (Bobbs-Merrill, 1939). The debate between Newton and Leibniz is played out in the *Leibniz-Clarke Correspondence*, where Samuel Clarke spoke for Newton. On the debate over the reality of past, present, and future; I recommend two essays, both in *Metaphysics* ed. Sider, Hawthorne, and Zimmerman (Blackwell, 2004). These are "The Privileged Present: Defending an A-Theory of Time" by Dean Zimmerman; and "The Tenseless Theory of Time" by J.J.C. Smart. Hilary Putnam's argument against presentism from relativity is "Time and Physical Geometry" from *The Journal of Philosophy* in 1967. Kristie Miller has a nice discussion of the three theories of time discussed here in her "Presentism, Eternalism, and the Growing Block" (*A Companion to the Philosophy of Time,* Wiley-Blackwell, 2013). See also her (with Sam Baron) *An Introduction to the Philosophy of Time* (Polity, 2018). L.A. Paul gives explanations of the feeling of temporal passage in "Temporal Experience" (Journal of Philosophy, 2010).

Question 7

IS TRUTH RELATIVE?

You might have wondered whether truth is in some way relative. We sometimes say things that might suggest it is. For instance, a professor might complain about incessant assessment meetings with administrators that take away from her teaching and research. A colleague might reply, "Well, it's all relative; you'd feel differently were you an administrator." Or we might say that relative to one person, using a neighbor's unsecured Wi-Fi rather than paying for one's own is wrong; relative to another person it is morally OK. Do these sorts of claims, and others like them, commit us to thinking that truth is relative in any robust sense? Precisely, what would truth's being relative entail or involve? We're going to examine these issues in this chapter. To begin, we'll try to get clear on what notion of "truth" we're employing when philosophers ask if truth can be relative. With some distinctions in hand, we then will look at the consequences of relativism about truth. We will close with some reflections about holding on to the notions and virtues that inspired relativism about truth in the first place.

What kinds of things are true?

We call all sorts of things true. There are things like true friends, true love, and true Chicago-style pizza. There also are things like true beliefs, true claims, and true statements. Sometimes, when we call something "true", we mean that it is real or genuine. I take it this is what occurs with "true" in the first group of things. We could replace "true" with "real" or "genuine" without significantly altering the meaning of the phrase (so "genuine friends", "genuine love", and "genuine Chicago-style pizza"). This doesn't work with the second group of things, though. If I say that what you believe is true, I'm not saying anything like that what you believe is genuine.

What am I saying, then, when I say that a belief, claim, or statement is true? This is a question that many philosophers have spent a great deal of time exploring. The answer that most philosophers settle on is something like this: A belief, claim, or statement is true if and only if it accurately represents the way things are. For instance, my belief that Los Angeles has more people than Chicago is true if and only if the way things are is such that Los Angeles has more people than Chicago. We then can call the *Correspondence Thesis* the claim that something X is true if and only if X accurately represents the way reality is.

So far we've talked about beliefs, claims, and statements being true. Are some of these true in virtue of others being true? Is there some kind of thing that is just true in some fundamental sense?

In attempting to answer this question, we can note that beliefs have a content, something they are about. If I believe that the sky is blue, there is something that is the content of my belief: that the sky is blue.

The same goes for claims and statements. If I claim or state that it is raining, there is something I claimed or stated: that it is raining.

Philosophers call the objects named by that-clauses (like those that-clauses above) *propositions*. Propositions are real, though non-concrete, objects that represent the world as being a particular way. They are the fundamental bearers of truth or falsity. This is to say that they aren't true or false because of their relations to assertions or claims or statements or beliefs. Why are they true or false, then? We can return to the Correspondence Thesis, and see that *a proposition p is true or false just in case p accurately represents the way reality is.*

With these concepts in mind, we can turn to a question that you may have wondered when you have thought about truth: Is truth relative?

a) Relativism and its Motivations

Relativism about truth is a view with a long history. In Western philosophy, its first articulation may have been from the ancient Greek philosopher Protagoras some 2,500 years ago when he said "man is the measure of all things." More recently, it is the sort of view that one might find espoused in many humanities classes in academia.

The thought that truth is relative can, on the face of it, seem appealing. There is a significant amount of disagreement in the world. For instance, some people think that the welfare state should be expanded to provide free college education to everyone who wants it. Others think that it shouldn't be so-expanded. Or, some people think that that there is just one thing—the universe—and it is divine. Other people think that the universe is a created thing and that God is separate from the universe. Still other people think that there is no God and that the universe is all that exists.

Thus, there is not homogeneity of beliefs about all sorts of different important matters. So it might be tempting to say something like the following about a case where I disagree with someone (say, about free college): Relative to *me*, the welfare state should be expanded to allow free college education to all who want it; relative to *you* it shouldn't be. This sounds respectful. We have started with what can be a contentious issue (the role of the welfare state often is), and we have given it a metaphysical patina designed to remove some of the contention. And in general we can do this. When there is an apparent contentious disagreement, we can remember that truth is relative and try to deal with the contention via this fact.

Why might relativism seem appealing in the face of disagreement? Perhaps the idea is that both parties can be right, in some sense, in their views about the contested issue. Let p be the proposition that abortion is morally permissible in some cases. Suppose Person A accepts p, and Person B denies p. We can say that both are right, relative to each of them. Relative to A, p is true. Relative to B, p is false. (I do not assert at this point that this view is *coherent*, only that it is the kind of thing a relativist about truth would like to say.)

It's not clear that this is the sort of thing most disputants would be happy with, though. I think that partisans with respect to a contentious issue (like the permissibility of abortion) think that they are right, *full stop*; and that those who deny the claim they believe are wrong, *full stop*. But right and wrong full stop is not consistent with relativism about truth.

What is truth relative *to* if it's relative? The best candidate here is that truth is relative to a set of *beliefs*. A proposition might true relative to what I believe, and false relative to what you believe. But what precisely does this mean? I take it this amounts to something like the following.

(RT) A proposition p *is true relative to the beliefs of a person S* if and only if: p is true because S believes that p.

And now we can define relativism about truth. *It is that every true proposition is true relative to some person*, as described in (RT).

It is worth noting that in some cases talk of relativism about truth can be misleading. For, sometimes when people appeal to the language of relativism in the face of disagreement, it is not clear they generally actually mean that propositions are true relative to particular subjects' beliefs (or anything else). Rather, what they mean is that there are different beliefs about the proposition in question. For instance, again suppose person A thinks that abortion is morally permissible in some cases. Person B thinks that abortion is never permissible. Someone might say, "Relative to A, abortion is morally permissible in some cases. Relative to B, it's not." But this may actually mean: "A believes abortion is permissible in some cases. B believes it never is." And when relative-to language is actually best understood as talk about differing beliefs (as certainly it sometimes is), we're not actually talking about truth being relative to beliefs. Indeed, this sort of language is consistent with A being right and B being wrong full stop (or vice versa).

b) Arguments Against Relativism About Truth

Very few contemporary philosophers are relativists about truth. This is because they take arguments against the view to be decisive. I want to state three of those objections here.

a) **The Multiple Realities Objection**: This objection starts with the observation that we interact with a shared, common reality. The world may *appear* different in some ways to me than it does to you. But in actuality, you and I interact with a common reality. Suppose that relativism about truth were true; suppose then for some proposition q, q is true for me and false for you. By the Correspondence Thesis, we know that q is true if and only if q accurately represents the way things are. So if q is true, then things are q-ish in reality. In particular, if q is true for me, then things are q-ish for me. Now, suppose q is false for you. Then things aren't q-ish for you. This seems to imply that you and I inhabit different realities or worlds—I a q world and you a not-q world. But reality is not divided between different people in this sort of way. We inhabit a shared, common reality. Therefore, relativism about truth is not correct.

b) **The Easy Truth Objection**: This objection is similar to the Many Realities Objection. The concern is this: Relativism makes it too easy to shape reality. According to our statement of truth being relative to me—(RT); if I believe p, then p is true for me. So if somehow I can get myself to believe certain propositions I really want to believe, then it will be true for me that things are that way. But surely this gets things wrong. I can't make most things true, even true relative to me (however one construes this), simply by believing it. Maybe a being like God can do this, but I cannot.

c) **Self-Referential Objection:** This is an objection that is designed to show that the relativist by her own lights isn't able to explain how anything could be relatively true. To see how it goes, recall our statement of truth's being relative to a person.

(**RT**) A proposition p *is true relative to the beliefs of a person S* if and only if: p is true because S believes that p.

The relativist, as we're thinking of her, thinks that all truth is relative truth in the sense given in (RT). But notice that in (RT) we're defining a proposition p's being true relative to a person in terms of its *being true* that the person believes p. What should we make of this "being true"? The relativist will insist that it itself is relative truth; all truth is relative truth. By (RT) we then know its truth holds in virtue of its being true some person S believing that it holds. But then we ask the same question about this new "being true" once again. At some point we arrive at a circumstance where there simply aren't subjects with the requisite beliefs to ground the ascription of relative truth. So, by the relativist's own theory nothing is relatively true.

These strike me, as they have many other philosophers, as very strong objections against relativism about truth. They suggest that relativism about truth cannot be correct.

c) Relativism: Concluding Thoughts

So it seems that relativism about truth doesn't work as a philosophical theory. What should someone who is attracted to the theory say, then? First, the relativist might recast her relativism in such a way that not all propositions are relatively true. One danger here is that the theory becomes *ad hoc* (Latin for unmotivated in its ungeneralizablity); why is this proposition true relatively, and this other one true non-relatively or absolutely? Second, the Multiple Realities and Easy Truth objections would remain for the person who weakens her relativism about truth in this sort of way.

Perhaps it is best to abandon relativism, then. But doesn't doing so commit one to a sort of dogmatism and intolerance? It might seem like this at first; recall that one reason someone might be drawn to relativism about truth is to preserve the idea that different sides in a dispute are right, in some sense. But it is consistent with the view that one disputant in a debate is right and the other wrong, that one shouldn't be intolerant and dogmatic. There presumably is a fact of the matter as to whether, for example, euthanasia is ever permissible. But there are well-informed and intelligent people on different sides of the euthanasia issue. So a natural position to adopt would be that, though *some* people hold false beliefs about the permissibility of euthanasia; no one is certain as to *which* people those are. Each party should be aware that she may well be wrong and the others in the dispute right. This, it would seem, should engender a non-dogmatic, tolerant attitude in the way one holds one's beliefs. We can allow for this without becoming relativists about truth.

Reflection Questions

1   What are propositions?

2   What is the Correspondence Thesis?

3   What is relativism about truth?

4   Why might someone be inclined to accept relativism about truth?

5   Which objection to relativism about truth do you find most compelling?

6   Can one be respectful of others who disagree with us even if we aren't relativists? How?

FURTHER READING:

Frederick Schmitt's *Truth: A Primer* (Westview, 1995). is an excellent introduction to philosophical thinking about the nature of truth. He has a nice discussion of relativism in chapter 2 of this book. More difficult but also excellent is William Alston's *A Realist Conception of Truth* (Cornell, 1997). He considers a view of Hilary Putnam's on which there are multiple realities in chapter 6. Putnam discusses his view that there are multiple realities that are dependent on the way we think in many places. One is in *Reason, Truth and History* (Cambridge, 1981), particularly in chapter 3. Maria Baghramian's "A Brief History of Relativism" in Michael Krausz ed. *Relativism: A Contemporary Anthology* (New York: Columbia) is a good account of the history of relativism. Tony Roy's short paper "Truth as Correspondence" is a good basic overview of truth and relativism.

Question 8

DOES PERCEPTION GIVE US KNOWLEDGE OF THE EXTERNAL WORLD?

When I was a child I watched many television shows about animals. I learned from one of these shows that dogs have different perceptions of color than humans do. So, when a dog and I both look at a rose; I see it as red, and he sees it as brownish. I remember being puzzled about this: "Which one of us is right? What if I'm wrong? What would that mean?" I don't think I had yet learned about human colorblindness when I wondered these things.

This sort of case is a part of a larger phenomenon that adults take for granted: There is a gap between appearance and reality. Things in the world appear to be ways they aren't. Once we realize this, it is natural to ask what the connection is between the things that are before the mind in sense perception, and the objects that exist independently of us in the world. Just a second ago I was looking at the table at which I am working. I had before my mind a brown, grainy expanse. Was that expanse the surface of the table? Or was the thing before my mind in perception actually a mental representation that in some way resembles the table out in the world?

Philosophers call that which is before my mind in cases of perception *the immediate object of perception*. The view on which the immediate objects of perception are things like surfaces of mind-independent objects is *direct realism*. (A mind-independent object is an object whose existence doesn't dependent on humans or other such minds.) The view on which the immediate objects of perception are wholly mental objects that resemble in some ways and are caused by objects in the world is *indirect realism*. Direct and indirect realism are *realist* views because each holds that there are mind-independent objects that we interact with in cases of sense perception.

Why might someone opt for one sort of realism over the other? One frequently sees cases of hallucination invoked as a way of supporting indirect realism. The standard argument goes something like this: There are cases of hallucination that appear just like cases of normal sense perception. The object of the hallucination is a wholly mental object. So we should think that in all cases of perception the immediate objects of perception are mental objects. As there are mind-independent objects, we should be indirect realists.

This strikes me as not a very good argument. Let's grant that there are wholly mental objects that we perceive in cases of hallucination. And let's grant the existence of cases where sensory experiences in the cases of hallucination are just like those in normal sensory perception. Why do they have to involve the same objects? Perhaps the immediate object of perception in the veridical case is a mind-independent object, even if the immediate object of perception in the hallucination case is a mental object. We need an argument for the claim that the immediate objects of perception in each case must be of the same kind. (The view that they involve different objects is called *disjunctivism.*)

Is there a better argument for indirect realism, then? There is, I think. This argument is often called the argument from perceptual relativity. It begins with a basic observation about the way things appear to us, and concludes that the immediate objects of perception aren't mind-independent objects in the world. If I walk around the table at which I am working, the immediate object of my perception changes color. It is a lighter brown in a particular region, and a darker brown in that region moments later. It is shinier on one part and then shinier on another part moments later. But the surface of the table in the world isn't changing colors just because I walk around it. So it can't be that the immediate object of perception is the surface of the table in the world. What sort of thing can change colors as I move around the table? A mental object that resembles the table and is caused by the table is exactly the sort of thing that could change colors in this fashion. But there is nothing special this particular case of sense perception. The appearances of physical objects change with changes in our perceptual circumstances all the time. Thus, the immediate objects of perception generally are mental objects. And, again, there clearly are mind-independent objects. Thus, indirect realism is true.

What should we think about this argument? One question you might have is about the inference from the fact that the immediate object of perception changes color and the table doesn't, to the conclusion that the immediate object of perception isn't the table. Why is this a good inference? This inference relies on a principle discussed in the appendix at the end of Question 1, *Leibniz's Law*. Leibniz's Law is the proposition that if some object A has a property that object B lacks, then A and B are distinct objects (that is, there are two of them). Leibniz's Law looks unimpeachable, so this inference looks to be solid.

Another question we might raise is about the statement that there is an object that is changing colors that is the immediate object of perception in this table case. Why think that? The words of British philosopher H.H. Price are relevant here. At the beginning of his 1932 book *Perception* he says:

> When I see a tomato there is much that I can doubt. I can doubt whether it is a tomato that I am seeing, and not a cleverly painted piece of wax. I can doubt whether there is any material thing there at all ... One thing however I cannot doubt: That there exists a red patch of a round and somewhat bulgy shape, standing out from a background of other color-patches, and having a certain visual depth, and that this whole field of color is directly present to my consciousness (3).

Just as it is obvious to Price that there is *something* before his mind that is red and bulgy; it is obvious to me that there is something before my mind that is changing color. Indeed, I am quite certain of this fact. I may not be able to discern anything for certain about what the world is like from the table-ish appearance I have. But there is an object there, before my mind, and it is changing color as I walk around the table. Of that much I am certain.

At this point, some will object that this reasoning is relying on the claim that if it appears to me as though there is something that is changing colors, then there is something that is changing colors. But all the time it can appear to us as though something exists, and we can be wrong. It can appear to me as though at night there is a person standing in my garden, and then I learn it's actually a hearty tomato plant. Or it can appear to me as though there is a spider on the wall, and then I learn it's actually a spot of paint. And so on. Isn't the form of inference here (if it appears to me as though there is something that is F (e.g., a person, a spider, etc.), then there really is something that is F-like) a bad inference form?

Defenders of the argument from perceptual relativity have insisted that it is important that one be clear about the sense of "appears" that is employed in the argument. It is obvious that it can appear or seem as though something exists, and it be false that that something exists. But the sort of appearance Price is talking about is a particular sort of appearance. It is the sort of appearance one has when one is immediately aware of an object. And as Price says, it is very hard to see how it can appear to me *in that sense* as though there is something, and there not be something that is as it appears to me to be. It might appear to him as though there exists a tomato, and there not be a tomato. But it can't be that there appears to be something *immediately before his mind* that is red and bulgy and there be no such thing. The senses of "appear" differ here, and that difference matters.

Suppose we're convinced that the argument from perceptual relativity is a good argument, and the immediate objects of perception are mental. And we're convinced there are mind-independent objects. Then, we're left to think that indirect realism is true. Most philosophers who are indirect realists have wanted to say that the mental objects immediately before our mind in sense perception resemble objects in the world in some ways, and not in others. We may divide the sorts of qualities those mental objects have into two categories. On the one hand, there are qualities like shape, size, motion, and extension. On the other hand, there are qualities like color, taste, and smell. Philosophers call the first sorts of qualities *primary qualities*, and the second *secondary qualities*. Most indirect realists think that mind-independent objects in the world have shapes, sizes, extensions, and the like. But they think that they don't have colors, tastes, and smells. That is, though things in the world resemble our perceptions' primary qualities; nothing in the world resembles our perceptions' secondary qualities. Things like colors and tastes don't exist out in the world, but only in our minds.

Why have philosophers split qualities into these two categories and said that the world contains only one category of them? It is thought that qualities like shape, size, and motion are more fundamental than qualities like color, taste, and smell. In order for there to be an object in the world that causes my perceptual experiences, it must have primary qualities. And it is its primary qualities' interacting with my sensory faculties that explain the sensory experience I have. To explain my sensory experience, there is no need to suppose that objects in the world have secondary qualities.

Some philosophers have thought that this sort of indirect realism implies skepticism about the external world. If the things immediately before my mind are mental, how can I tell if they properly represent the material objects in the world that are independent of my mind? The mental objects before my mind in perception form a sort of curtain between me and the objects in the world. I'm not able to step back and see whether the curtain matches the world behind it. So if indirect realism is true, I have no knowledge of the external world.

One philosopher who reasoned in this way was the fascinating eighteenth-century Irish philosopher George Berkeley. Berkeley had several arguments that if indirect realism were true, that we couldn't know anything about the external world. One of them was the argument in the last paragraph. Berkeley claimed not to be a skeptic, though. And he didn't adopt direct realism, as he thought it was shown to be false by considerations of perceptual relativity. How then did he manage to avoid skepticism? Notice that at the end of the argument from perceptual relativity for indirect realism is an assertion of realism: "clearly there are mind-independent objects." But Berkeley wondered, why should we think *that*? Why can't we accept the argument up to its end and avoid the realism?

Much of Berkeley's metaphysics was a reaction to that of the English philosopher John Locke, who was born fifty-three years before Berkeley. Locke himself was an indirect realist, and he too grappled with the question of why we should think there are mind-independent objects. He noted that the ideas and images that come to me in sensory perception aren't conjured up by me. They occur regardless of my will. I am a passive recipient of them. He also noted that these ideas and images form a coherent whole, in the way that they don't in the case of dreams. Locke thought that the best explanation of these two facts about perceptual ideas and images is that there are mind-independent objects in the world that human beings perceive in common.

Berkeley thought that there was a better explanation of these two facts about ideas and images from perception. He argued in various ways that mind-independent objects of a Lockean ilk couldn't produce in us these ideas and images. What could explain the coherence and spontaneity of perceptual ideas and images, then? Berkeley thought the best explanation of them was that a good God that caused perceptual ideas and images in each of us and coordinated them between different people. There is no need for mind-independent objects to explain sensory perceptions on Berkeley's model. Indeed, Berkeley went further; he thought that the idea of a mind-independent object was incoherent. Rather than a Lockean sort of reality populated with mind-independent objects causing ideas in various human minds, Berkeley thought that reality consisted entirely of minds and ideas of various sorts. One of these minds is God. Others are human minds.

The view of Berkeley's is called *idealism*. It might seem to you that idealism clearly is false. Can't we demonstrate conclusively that there are mind-independent objects? I'm touching a computer right now, and also sitting in a chair. I'm able to perceive these mind-independent objects. So they must exist. (Famously, the eighteenth-century English intellectual Samuel Johnson replied to Berkeley's idealism by kicking a rock and shouting "I refute him thus!")

If idealism were true, however, things would look exactly as they do to me right now. I would feel the solidity of a chair and the warmth of a computer keyboard. I would taste the bitterness of a lemon and see the greenness of leaves on a tree. I could kick a rock and feel its hardness and a pain in my foot. The source of these perceptual ideas would be God, rather than mind-independent objects. But from my point of view things would look exactly the same. (This should remind you of the discussion of the second premise of our skeptical argument in chapter 4.)

Let's return to questions of skepticism. How does Berkeley avoid the sort of skepticism he sees arising on indirect realism? In short, he denies that there are mind-independent objects to be skeptical about. If one is concerned about getting beyond the curtain of ideas and images to have knowledge of mind-independent objects in the world, one strategy is to deny that there are any such objects!

It is worth asking whether the indirect realist actually is in particularly difficult circumstances vis-à-vis skepticism. This arises from the picture of the curtain of sense perceptions lying between us and mind-independent objects in the world. But this is just a picture, and perhaps an unhelpful (though common) one. The direct realist too has to allow for a gap between appearance and reality. (How the idealist does this is, as you might imagine, a tricky question.) Once one allows that the way things appear to one may differ from how they are, and that one can't "independently" compare how things appear and how they are; one is left with potential skepticism about the external world. This isn't a worse problem for the indirect realist than for the direct realist, though. Both face the same problem. So there may be reasons to adopt direct realism over indirect realism, but avoiding skepticism isn't one of them.

Reflection Questions

1　What is indirect realism?

2　What is direct realism?

3　What is idealism?

4   Why might indirect realism be thought to lead to skepticism?

5   How does Berkeley avoid skepticism that he thinks indirect realism engenders?

6   Which do you find most plausible, and why: indirect realism, direct realism, idealism?

FURTHER READING

The classic statement of an argument for indirect realism from perceptual relativity is in chapter 1 of Bertrand Russell's *The Problems of Philosophy* from 1912. Howard Robinson's *Perception* (Routledge, 2003) is an excellent introduction to issues in the philosophy of perception. Berkeley states his views in his *Three Dialogues* and his *Principles*. Locke states his views in his *Essay Concerning Human Understanding*. Berkeley is a reasonably clear writer, and you should be able to pick up his work and understand it. Locke is not a clear writer, so be patient with yourself with him. The introduction in Tamar Szábo Gendler and John Hawthorne's *Perceptual Experience* (Oxford, 2006) is a good more contemporary introduction to the nature of perceptual experience and representation.

Question 9

WHAT ARE FICTIONAL CHARACTERS?

Imagine the following conversation.

Person 1: "Javert [a character from *Les Miserables*] lives in England."
Person 2: "No, Javert lives in France."
Person 3 (who is a philosophy student): "You're both wrong. Javert doesn't exist. So he doesn't live anywhere."

You may feel a pull in the direction of the statements of either Person 2 or Person 3. Indeed, you may feel a pull in the direction of each of them. If someone asked you to make a list of all that there is, you'd not include Javert on it, right? On the other hand, surely there is something correct about saying that he lives in Paris rather than London. But how could that be if he doesn't exist?

We putatively talk about fictional characters all the time. Yet, if you pause to think about this talk, it can quickly seem very puzzling. Are there (in any sense) fictional characters? If there are, where do they come from? If there aren't, how do we make sense of our talk about fiction?

In this chapter we're going to consider some different views about the metaphysics of fictional characters. In the last forty years, philosophers have devoted a great deal of time to thinking about issues around fictional characters. In light of this work, we will set out some competing views and reasons why one might think each view is true, or false.

We begin our discussion by noting two different kinds of existing objects: concrete and abstract. (In chapter 8 we noted that propositions are examples of objects that aren't concrete.) It is tough to say exactly what makes something a concrete object as opposed to an abstract object. We can, however, give a list of clear examples of each. Concrete objects include things like tables, chairs, planets, atoms, and animals. Abstract objects include things like numbers, properties, relations, and sets. We can note that abstract objects are not the sort of thing that one finds located in space and time. So, regardless how hard you search; you never will find the number 4 anywhere. You will find the *numeral* '4' many places: On signs, whiteboards, and receipts, among others. You also will find collections of four things: The Beatles, the Gospels, and seasons, among others. But you won't find the number four itself anywhere. This is an indication that we should think of it as an abstract object. By contrast, concrete objects—things like tables, chairs, planets, atoms, animals—*are* located in space and time.

You might be inclined to think that we should just identify abstract objects with nonspatial and nontemporal objects, and concrete objects with objects located in space and time. But that's not quite right. If there is a God or there are beings like angels, they aren't located in space. Nor are immaterial minds of the sort discussed in chapter 2. But all these sorts of things are concrete.

Fictional characters are, in this regard like the number four. If they exist, they aren't to be found in concrete reality. There may be people who *resemble* fictional characters. For instance, a person at work may resemble Scrooge, or Captain Queeg. Or someone working at the amusement park may resemble Harry Potter. But you never will encounter a fictional character in day-to-day life. This is true regardless of how hard you search for one. If they exist, they aren't to be found in ordinary, concrete reality.

This fact will constrain the sorts of views of fictional characters that we will consider. If fictional characters exist, they must not be concrete objects. They must be abstract.

We're going to divide the views we will consider into two camps: Those on which fictional characters exist, and those on which they don't. We begin with views on which fictional characters exist. We will first state the various views we will consider, and then will consider what we should think of the truth of the different positions.

Views on which fictional objects exist

1 **Creationism about fictional characters.** According to creationism about fictional characters, fictional characters exist and are created by human beings. A creationist about fictional characters might say the fictional character Harry Potter exists and was created by J.K. Rowling. Other sorts of characters may be created by multiple people. This may be the case with fictional stories with multiple authors, or with stories

that are started by one person and continued by another (such as with Game of Thrones).

2 Discoverism about fictional characters. According to the discoverist about fictional characters, fictional characters exist prior to the writing or creation of a fiction. They are then picked out by the creator of the fiction when the fiction is written down or told. On this view, J.K. Rowling refers to an already-existing fictional character when she writes about Harry Potter in the Harry Potter stories. How does she do this? Presumably, she begins with a description (an English boy wizard with a scar on his forehead and round glasses, etc.), and this description picks out a particular fictional character.

There is a famous anecdote about Michelangelo; who said that before he carved a sculpture from a block of marble, the statue was already there in the block. He just needed to get rid of the bits of stone obscuring the statue. On one way of interpreting Michelangelo, he was discovering, rather than creating the statue. The discoverist about fictional characters thinks something similar about fictional characters. When someone writes down a work of fiction, they pick from already-existing fictional objects and tell stories about those objects.

Views on which fictional objects don't exist

1 Meinongianism about fictional characters. The early twentieth-century philosopher Alexius Meinong is famous among philosophers for his claim that there are things that don't exist. Among these are fictional characters. We should be clear on what we're saying when we consider the claim that there are things that don't exist. We aren't saying there *exist* things that don't exist. That doesn't make any sense. Rather, those who follow Meinong typically claim that reality encompasses more than just those things that exist. Everything that exists is part of reality, but not everything that is part of reality exists. So when we consider the claim "There are things that don't exist", we should read it as saying "There are (in a maximally broad sense) things that don't exist." The Meinongian about fictional characters thinks there are fictional characters like Harry Potter. Harry Potter doesn't exist, but there is (in a maximally broad sense) such a thing as Harry Potter. He is a concrete, nonexistent object.

2   A truth-in-fiction theory. On what we will call the truth-in-fiction view, terms like "Harry Potter" don't refer to anything, existent or nonexistent. Sentences like "Harry Potter is a wizard" come out false, as there is (in a maximally broad sense) nothing that "Harry Potter" picks out. But a sentence very close to this sentence is true: "In the Harry Potter fiction, Harry Potter is a wizard." Philosophers who favor this approach will then proceed to give an account of what it is for a sentence to be true in a fiction. Usually this account will include saying what a fiction is. For our purposes, we can consider a fiction to be a set of propositions (recall again our discussion of propositions in chapter 8). Then, roughly, for a sentence to be true in a fiction is for the proposition that the sentence expresses to be a member of the set that is a particular fiction. So the Harry Potter fiction is a set of propositions. The sentence "Harry Potter is a wizard" is true in the Harry Potter fiction if and only if the proposition expressed by the sentence "Harry Potter is a wizard" is a member of the set that is the Harry Potter fiction.

Evaluation of the Views

Each of these four views have distinguished defenders. What should we think of each of them? With respect to creationism about fictional characters, one might be concerned with our ability to create abstract objects. We don't typically create abstract objects. (Objection: "But what about sets? I create the set having as members these two sandwiches by creating the sandwiches." Reply: "I do create the sandwiches. And as a result the set with the sandwiches as members comes to be. But I don't create the set, at least not in the way the creationist thinks we create fictional characters.") There is a perhaps similar sort of concern for the discoverist. The discoverist thinks that there are many already-existing abstract fictional characters, and the fictional author picks one out and describes it. But how does this work? There are presumably *a lot* of already-existing fictional characters. We say that Harry Potter could have had long hair, or no hair, or two scars on his forehead, or a scar shaped like a triangle on his forehead. Had Rowling conceived Harry Potter in any of these ways, presumably she then would have been writing about a different fictional character. That much seems fine. But there will be many different fictional characters that fit Rowling's description of Harry Potter. Why is this? Because no fictional writer gives a fine-grained enough description to pick out just one fictional character. Had Rowling given a more complete description of Harry Potter, she'd have ruled out some of the many candidates for Harry Potter that are consistent with her actual description. But there still would be many consistent with the new, more-complete description. How, then, does the author wind up writing about just one of these fictional objects?

Suppose one can find solutions to these two objections to views on which fictional characters are abstract objects of some sort. There is another, even more serious objection to these two views. That is that fictional objects, as abstract objects, don't have the properties they are said to have. No abstract object is a wizard. Only concrete objects can be a wizard. No abstract object wears glasses. Only concrete objects wear glasses. And so on. The whole point of saying that fictional characters were existing, abstract objects was for there to be something the authors are talking about when they make reference to fictional characters' having various attributes. But the sorts of things that authors talk about on these first two views make their claims about fictional characters come out false.

At this point, defenders of creationism and discoverism tend to invoke a distinction between two different ways whereby a fictional object may relate to properties. For instance, the philosopher Peter van Inwagen says that fictional objects can *have* properties and can *hold* properties. Fictional objects *have* properties like *being a fictional object* or *being an abstract object*. That is, having is the normal relation we think of as existing between a property and something that has or exemplifies that property. Fictional objects, on the other hand, *hold* properties like, *being a wizard*, and *wearing round glasses*. Other defenders of creationism and discoverism incorporate distinctions that functionally mirror van Inwagen's have/hold distinction. We can quickly figure out which properties a fictional character is supposed to hold and not hold—it holds those that it has in the story, and doesn't hold those it doesn't. Harry Potter holds *being a wizard* and doesn't hold *being an NBA power forward*. But there remains a problem here, in that most of the characterizing of fictional characters comes out false. It is not enough to say that there is this other, unexplicated way in which fictional characters relate to properties. According to this approach, it still is false that Harry Potter is a wizard, and true that he is an abstract object. Both of these results tell strongly against the view that Harry Potter is an abstract object, created or discovered.

Suppose we are moved by these criticisms of the first views. Then we're left with two views on which it is false that fictional characters exist. The difference between these views centers on whether a term like "Harry Potter" picks out anything at all or not. The Meinongian thinks that it does—it picks out a nonexistent object. The truth-in-fiction theorist thinks that it doesn't pick out anything. How should we decide between these two views? Suppose you are inclined to think, as I do, that there aren't (in any sense of "are") any nonexistent objects. Then you will be inclined in the direction of the truth-in-fiction view. Some philosophers think that there aren't nonexistent objects because they think that the concept of a nonexistent object is incoherent. I have some sympathy for this view. Now, it is not incoherent to say there are objects that don't exist in quite the way it is incoherent to say, e.g., that there are female bachelors. One quickly can deduce a contradiction from the plain meanings of the terms in the sentence "there are female bachelors." But I do struggle to make sense of the claim that there are things that don't exist. I must weigh this against the fact that some very able philosophers—philosophers for whom I have a great deal of respect—*do* think there are objects that don't exist. I thus am reluctant to pound on the table and assert loudly that any view that includes nonexistent objects doesn't make sense. But accepting nonexistent objects strikes me as a cost for a view. Indeed, it is a cost that I would prefer to avoid if I could.

Another concern for the view on which fictional characters are nonexistent objects parallels a concern we saw for the discoverist. There are (in as broad a sense as the Meinongian wants) presumably very many indeed nonexistent boy wizards with all the properties set out in the Harry Potter books. How does J.K. Rowling come to write about one of them in particular? How is one of them picked out from all the other nonexistent boy wizards?

On the other hand, the truth-in-fiction view looks more promising to me. It accounts for what a writer or creator of fiction does (she picks out a set of propositions that will be the fiction). It gives a general account of what it is for a proposition to be true in a fiction (it is e.g., just membership in the set of propositions that is the fiction). There are important details to be filled in with the truth-in-fiction account, however. What about claims that the author never explicitly asserts? Suppose Harry Potter is riding a dragon, and J.K. Rowling doesn't say how many spines the dragon has on its back. Presumably there is still some fact of the matter as to how many spines the dragon has on its back. Which proposition about dragon spines gets included in the set? (There will be many, many such propositions. Even the most detail-oriented author leaves out many details of a story.) So there will be problems for the truth-in-fiction view that are akin to those for the discoverist and the Meinongian: There will be many candidates for being the set of propositions that is the fiction, and there will need to be some sort of account on which the author settles on a particular set as the story she is telling.

Here is another question for the truth-in-fiction view. Doesn't it suffer from the same problem the discoverist and creationist views do: On it, isn't it false that Harry Potter is a wizard? Yes, it is. But the defender of the truth-in-fiction view can point to a claim very close to this which *is* true, which is that *in Harry Potter stories, Harry Potter is a wizard*. Indeed, if you stop and think about the claim that Harry Potter is a wizard, it may seem puzzling to you. How could he be a wizard if Harry Potter isn't any sort of thing at all? How could Harry Potter have any attributes if he isn't an existent or a nonexistent thing? Thus, I think there is something for the truth-in-fiction theorist to say here to the criticism that ordinary sentences of fiction come out false on her view.

Overall, then, I think there is reason to think that names like "Harry Potter", when used in a fictional way, don't refer to anything, existent or nonexistent. But there are true claims that one makes about the Harry Potter story, in particular that according to it Harry Potter is a wizard. There is much more to be said about all of these views, however. Philosophers at this very moment are trying to get clear on the nature of fictional characters, if there are (in any sense of "are") such things.

Reflection Questions

1   What are some examples of concrete objects? Abstract objects?

2   What is creationism about fictional characters?

3   What is discoverism about fictional characters?

4 What is Meinongianism about fictional characters?

5 What is the truth-in-fiction view of fictional characters?

6 Which of the above views do you find most plausible,
   and why?

FURTHER READING

The truth-in-fiction view is sketched in chapter 8 of Alvin
Plantinga's *The Nature of Necessity* (Oxford, 1974). Two widely-
read papers on fictional characters are Peter van Inwagen's
"Creatures of Fiction" (*American Philosophical Quarterly*, 1977)
and David Lewis' "Truth in Fiction," (*American Philosophical
Quarterly*, 1978). Both are hard for someone new to philosophy,
particular Lewis' paper. Amie Thomasson is perhaps the most
prominent contemporary defender of a creationist view. See her
Fiction and Metaphysics (Cambridge, 2008). R.M. Sainsbury's
Fiction and Fictionalism (Routledge, 2010) gives a nice overview of
different theories of fiction.

WHERE TO GO NEXT?

Suppose after reading this book, you wanted further reading in philosophy. There are many good general philosophy anthologies. Two that I like are:

Exploring Philosophy ed. Stephen Cahn (Oxford University Press). I often use this in my introductory courses. It has a wide selection of excerpted philosophical texts.

Reason and Responsibility eds. Joel Feinberg and Russ Schafer-Landau (Wadsworth). This text has been around a long time (I used it in my introduction to philosophy course!). It's a really thorough reader. Older editions of the text are often found cheap online.

Or suppose after reading this book—which is focused on metaphysics and epistemology—you wanted to read some more metaphysics or epistemology. There are many excellent introductory texts in metaphysics and epistemology. Here are a few that I recommend. The list is in order of difficulty, with the easiest at the top of each category.

Metaphysics:

1 *Metaphysics* by Peter van Inwagen, (Routledge, 2014).

As you've seen in the course of this book, van Inwagen is an important contemporary metaphysical thinker. The book is aimed at people who have not done metaphysics before, and has nice discussions of free will and the question of why is there something rather than nothing.

2 *Metaphysics: An Introduction* by Alyssa Ney, (Routledge, 2014).

This is an exceptionally clear general introduction to metaphysics. Unlike most such books, it includes a discussion of the metaphysics of race.

3 *Metaphysics* by Michael J. Loux and Thomas M. Crisp, (Routledge, 2017).

This is a hard, though really impressive treatment of debates in contemporary metaphysics.

Epistemology:

1 *On Epistemology* by Linda Zagzebski, (Wadsworth, 2009).

This is a clear, accessible introduction to the theory of knowledge with a focus on the role of intellectual virtues in knowing. Zagzebski is the leading thinker in this field, which is called "virtue epistemology."

2 *Epistemology: A Contemporary Introduction to the Theory of Knowledge* by Robert Audi, (Routledge, 2011).

This is a moderately-difficult very comprehensive text aimed at people taking a first epistemology class.

3   *Epistemology* by Richard Feldman, (Prentice Hall, 2002).

This is slightly more difficult than Audi's book. It is really clear and precise; I often use it in my epistemology classes for this reason.

4   *Evidence and Inquiry* by Susan Haack, (Blackwell, 1995).

A really important book by a leading logician and epistemologist. She tries to steer a middle path between two prominent schools of contemporary epistemology, and in doing so illuminates the nature of the debate between them.

5   *Contemporary Theories of Knowledge* by John L. Pollock and Joseph Cruz, (Rowman and Littlefield, 1999).

This is the hardest of the five. It is the text used in my first epistemology class, and I remember working hard to understand what was said in it. But it is comprehensive, clear, and fair; and is really an excellent text to read after you've read some of the other books in the list.

GLOSSARY

Absolutism about time the view that there can be time without change.

Abstract objects objects that are not concrete. Examples include properties, relations, propositions, sets, and numbers.

Agent causation a unique sort of causation that occurs between an agent and an action.

Argument an argument is a series of statements (premises) that are intended to support another statement (conclusion).

Baker, Lynne Rudder (1944–2017) an American philosopher who thinks that human persons are material objects constituted by our bodies.

Berkeley, George (1685–1753) an Irish philosopher who argued that there are no mind-independent material objects.

Boethius an early medieval philosopher who argued that God is outside of time.

Chisholm, Roderick (1916–1999) an American metaphysican and epistemologist who argued for agent causation.

Consequence argument an argument for incompatibilism. This is discussed in chapter 5.

Compatibilism the view that it's possible for actions to be determined by the past and the laws of nature and still be free.

Concrete objects ordinary objects of the sort we encounter in ordinary life. Some examples include tables, chairs, dogs, and other people.

Correspondence thesis the view that things are true in virtue of correctly representing the way reality is.

Creationism about fictional characters the view that fictional characters exist and are created by storytellers.

Descartes, René (1596–1650) a French philosopher and mathematician who argued that the self is an immaterial mind.

Determinism the view that given the past and the laws of nature, only one future is possible.

Direct realism the view that there are objects that exist independently of minds, and the immediate object of perception when we perceive them is mind-independent (e.g., the surfaces of objects that we see). The direct realist typically will say that objects we perceive have both primary and secondary qualities.

Discoverism about fictional characters the view that fictional characters exist independently of storytellers, and a storyteller picks individual characters out in the course of telling stories.

Disjunctivism the view that the immediate object of perception normally is something mind-independent (like the surface of an object that is seen), and the immediate object of perception in cases of hallucination is mind-dependent (like an image of some sort).

Easy truth objection an objection to relativism about truth. The objection is that if relativism were true, we could change reality just by changing our beliefs.

Epistemology the study of the nature of knowledge.

Eternal god is eternal just if God is outside of time and isn't subject to temporal change.

Eternalism the view that all past and future objects are just as real as present objects.

The Experience Machine a philosophical thought experiment designed to test whether pleasure (and more generally the way things appear to you) is what is good. It was created by Robert Nozick.

Goldman, Alvin a contemporary epistemologist who argues that in order to have knowledge we need to rule out only relevant alternatives in which our beliefs are false.

Growing block theory the view that the past and present are real, but the future isn't. As time passes, the present is added to the "block" that includes past events and things.

Hume, David (1711–1776) a Scottish philosopher who argued for skepticism about the external world and the self.

Idealism the view that there are no objects that exist independently of minds. This view was famously held by George Berkeley.

Immediate object of perception the thing that is immediately before the mind when sense perception occurs. For example, the direct realist will say that when I see a table, the immediate object of perception is the surface of the table.

Indirect realism the view that there are objects that exist independently of minds, and that the immediate object of perception when we perceive them is mind-dependent. The indirect realist typically will say that mind-independent objects we perceive have only primary qualities.

Incompatibilism the view that if an action is determined by the past and the laws of nature it is not free.

Indeterminism the view that given the past and the laws of nature, multiple futures are possible.

Leibniz, Gottfried (1646–1716) a German philosopher and mathematician who argued that space and time are relational.

Leibniz's Law the view that if some object x is identical with some object y, x and y have all the same properties.

Locke, John (1632–1704) an English philosopher who argued that the immediate objects of our perception are mental items (he called them "ideas") that resemble in some ways objects in the world.

McTaggard, J.M.E. (1866–1955) an English philosopher who argued that time is unreal.

Metaphysics the study of the fundamental nature of reality.

Meinong, Alexius (1853–1920) an Austrian philosopher who argued that there are objects that are being and existence.

Meinongianism about fictional characters the view that fictional characters are concrete objects that don't exist.

Momentarily-Lasting Person Stage a person that lasts only for a moment of time.

Monotheism the view that there is one divine being or God.

Moore, G.E. (1873–1958) an English philosopher who argued that skepticism could be refuted by the obvious truth of claims to know basic things about the world (e.g., that here is a hand).

Multiple realities objection an objection to relativism about truth. It is that if relativism were true, each of us would inhabit different realities.

Newton, Issac (1643–1727) an English scientist and philosopher who developed Newtonian physics. He also argued that time and space are absolute.

Nozick, Robert (1938–2002) a political philosopher who argued for libertarianism in political philosophy as well as devised the experience machine thought experiment.

Ockhamism the view that free creatures have the ability to act in such a way that God would have had different beliefs about the past. This is a way to try to reconcile divine foreknowledge of human actions and human free will.

Omnicompetent a being is omnicompetent if and only if it is omniscient, perfectly good, and, omnipotent.

Omnipotent a being is omnipotent if and only if it is all powerful.

Omniscient a being is omnipotent if and only if it knows all truths.

Open theism the view that God doesn't know what free creatures will do. Rather, God knows only probabilities as to how free creatures will act.

Parmenides a presocratic philosopher (alive around 500 BCE) who argued that reality consists in just one object that doesn't undergo temporal change.

Perfect-Being theology reasoning that begins from the idea that God is the greatest possible being, and draws inferences about God's attributes from it.

Presentism the view that there are no wholly past or future objects.

Primary qualities examples include shape, figure, extension, and solidity. They are thought to be more fundamental than secondary qualities.

Principle of sufficient reason the claim that for any truth, there is a sufficient reason why it is true.

Prior, Arthur (1914–1969) a philosopher and logician who argued for presentism.

Propositions abstract objects that are the fundamental bearers of truth and falsity. They are expressed by ordinary declarative sentences.

Protagoras a presocratic Greek philosopher (he lived in the sixth century BCE) who is famous for giving a statement of relativism, "man is the measure of all things."

Quantum mechanics the branch of physics that studies the behavior of very small objects like atoms and parts of atoms. It sometimes is taken to imply that determinism is false.

Quine, W. V. (1908–2000) a philosopher and logician who argued that philosophy, properly done, is continuous with science.

Relationalism about time the view that there can't be temporal passage without change.

Relativism about truth the view that every proposition is true relative to some person.

Realism the view that there are objects that exist independently of minds.

Revealed theology truths about God that we learn from sources like holy scripture or the testimony of holy people (such as prophets).

Rollback argument an argument that indeterminism is incompatible with free will. This is discussed in chapter 5.

Secondary qualities these include taste, smell, warmth, and color. They are typically thought to be dependent on primary qualities in some sort of way.

Self-Referential objection to relativism the objection that relativism about truth can't be true by its own lights.

Sempiternal god is sempiternal just if God exists at every time and is subject to temporal change.

Soundness an argument is sound if and only if (i) it is valid and (ii) it has true premises.

Stine, Gale (1940–1977) an American epistemologist who argues that in order to have knowledge we need to rule out only relevant alternatives in which our beliefs are false.

Thomasson, Amie an American philosopher who is a creationist about fictional characters.

Thought experiments they are used by philosophers to test the truth of philosophical claims. One example of this is Robert Nozick's Experience Machine.

Validity an argument is valid if and only if it is not possible for its premises to be true while its conclusion is false.

Van Inwagen, Peter a currently-working metaphysician who has defended libertarianism in free will and creationism about fictional characters.

BIBLIOGRAPHY

Alexander, R.G. ed. 1956, *The Leibniz-Clarke Correspondence*, Manchester: Manchester University Press.

Aristotle. 1975, *Categories and De Interpretatione*, trans. J.L. Ackrill, Oxford: Oxford University Press.

Audi, Robert. 2011, *Epistemology: A Contemporary Introduction to the Theory of Knowledge*, New York: Routledge.

Alston, William. 1997, *A Realist Conception of Truth*, Ithaca: Cornell University Press.

Baghramian, Maria. 2010, "A Brief History of Relativisms," in *Relativism: A Contemporary Anthology*, ed. Michael Krausz, (New York: Columbia).

Baker, Lynne Rudder. 2000, *Persons and Bodies: A Constitution View*, Cambridge: Cambridge University Press.

Baron, Sam and Kristie Miller. 2019, *An Introduction to the Philosophy of Time*, Cambridge: Polity.

Bealer, George. 1999, "A Theory of the A Priori." *Philosophical Perspectives* 13, pp. 29–55.

Berkeley, George. 1901, *Three Dialogues Between Hylas and Philonous*, Chicago: Open Court.

BonJour, Lawrence. 1998, *In Defense of Pure Reason*, Cambridge: Cambridge University Press.

Cornford, Francis MacDonald. 1939, *Plato and Parmenides*, Indianapolis: Bobbs-Merrill.

Descartes, René. 1913, *The Meditations and Selections from the Principles*, tr. John Veitch, Chicago: Open Court.

Dretske, Fred. 2013, "The Case Against Closure," in Steup, Matthias; Sosa, Ernest; and Turri, John, eds. *Contemporary Debates in Epistemology* 2nd ed. Oxford: Blackwell.

Ekstrom, Laura. 2011, "Free will is Not a Mystery," *The Oxford Handbook of Free Will*, ed. Robert Kane, Oxford: Oxford University Press.

Feldman, Richard. 2003, *Epistemology*, Upper Saddle River: Prentice Hall.

Gendler, Tamar Szábo; and Hawthorne, John eds. 2006, *Perceptual Experience*, Oxford: Oxford.

Gertler, Brie. 2002, "Can Feminists be Cartesians?" *Dialogue* XLI, pp. 91–112.

Goldman, Alvin. 1976, "Discrimination and Perceptual Knowledge," *Journal of Philosophy*, Vol. 73, No. 20, pp. 771–91.

Haack, Susan. 1996, *Evidence and Inquiry: Towards Reconstruction in Epistemology*, Oxford: Blackwell.

Hawthorne, John. 2013, "The Case for Closure," in Steup, Matthias; Sosa, Ernest; and Turri, John, eds. *Contemporary Debates in Epistemology* 2nd ed. Oxford: Blackwell.

Hume, David. 1978. *A Treatise on Human Nature*, 2nd ed. ed. P.H. Nidditch, Oxford: Oxford University Press.

Kane, Robert. 2005, *A Contemporary Introduction to Free Will*, Oxford: Oxford University Press.

Levin, Janet. 2005, "The Evidential Status of Philosophical Intuitions," *Philosophical Studies* (no. 121, pp. 193–224)

Lewis, David. 1978, "Truth in Fiction," in *American Philosophical Quarterly*, Vol. 15, No. 1, pp. 37–46.

Luper, Steven. 2013, "Cartesian Skepticism," in *The Routledge Companion to Epistemology*, eds. Sven Bernecker and Duncan Pritchard, New York: Routledge.

Locke, John. 1975, *An Essay Concerning Human Understanding*, ed. P.H. Nidditch, Oxford: Oxford University Press.

Loux, Michael J. and Crisp, Thomas M. 2017, *Metaphysics*, New York: Routledge.

Martin, Raymond and Barresi, John, eds. 2002, *Personal Identity*, Oxford: Blackwell.

Maudlin, Tim. 2011, *Quantum Non-Locality and Relativity: Metaphysical Intimations of Modern Physics*, Hoboken: Wiley-Blackwell.

Miller, Kristie. "Presentism, Eternalism, and the Growing Block," in *A Companion to the Philosophy of Time*, ed. Heather Dyke and Adrian Bardon, 2013, Hoboken: Wiley-Blackwell.

Moore, G.E. 1993, "Proof of an External World," *Selected Writings*, ed. Thomas Baldwin, New York: Routledge.

Ney, Alyssa. 2014, *Metaphysics An Introduction*, New York: Routledge.

Nozick, Robert. 1974, *Anarchy, State, and Utopia*, New York: Basic Books.

Olson, Erik. 2007, *What Are We? A Study in Personal Ontology*, Oxford: Oxford University Press.

Parfit, Derek. 1986, *Reasons and Persons*, Oxford: Oxford University Press.

Paul, L.A., 2010, "Temporal Experience," *The Journal of Philosophy*, Vol. CVII, No. 7, pp. 333–59.

Perry, John, ed. 2008, *Personal Identity*, Berkeley: University of California Press.

Pinnock, Clark, et al. eds. 1994, *The Openness of God* (Downers Grove: InterVarsity Press).

Plantinga, Alvin. 1974, *The Nature of Necessity*, Oxford: Clarendon Press.

Plato. 2002, *Euthyphro*, in *Five Dialogues*, trans. G.M.A. Grube, rev. John M. Cooper, Indianapolis: Hackett.

Pollock John L. and Cruz, Joseph. 1999, *Contemporary Theories of Knowledge* (Lanham: Rowman and Littlefield).

Price, H.H. 1932, *Perception*, London: Methuen.

Putnam, Hilary. 1967, "Time and Physical Geometry," *The Journal of Philosophy*, Vol. 64, No. 8, pp. 240–47.

Putnam, Hilary. 1981, *Reason, Truth, and History*, Cambridge: Cambridge University Press.

Quine, W.V. 1969, "Epistemology Naturalized," in *Ontological Relativity*, New York: Columbia.

Rorty, Amélie Oksenberg, ed. 1976, *The Identities of Persons*, Berkeley: University of California Press.

Roy, Tony. 2003, "Truth as Correspondence," from https://tonyroyphilosophy. net/wp-content/uploads/2019/03/truth.pdf retrieved July 2020.

Russell, Bertrand. 1912, *The Problems of Philosophy*, New York: Henry Holt and Company.

Sainsbury, R.M. 2010, *Fiction and Fictionalism*, New York: Routledge.

Schechtman, Mayra. 2007, *The Constitution of Selves*, Ithaca: Cornell University Press.

Schmitt, Frederick. 1995, *Truth: A Primer*, Boulder: Westview.

Sider, Theodore; Hawthorne, John; and Zimmerman, Dean (eds.). 2004. *Metaphysics*, Oxford: Blackwell.

Smart, J.J.C. 2004, "The Tenseless Theory of Time," in Sider et al.

Speak, Daniel. 2011, "The Consequence Argument Revisited," in *The Oxford Handbook of Free Will*, ed. Robert Kane, Oxford: Oxford University Press.

Stine, Gail. 1976, "Skepticism, Relevant Alternatives, and Deductive Closure," *Philosophical Studies*, Vol. 29, No. 4 (Apr., 1976), pp. 249–61.

Steup, Matthias; Sosa, Ernest; and Turri, John, eds. 2013, *Contemporary Debates in Epistemology* 2nd ed. Oxford: Blackwell.

Stump, Eleonore. 2016, *The God of the Bible and the God of the Philosophers*, Milwaukee: Marquette.

Thomasson, Amie. 2008, *Fiction and Metaphysics*, Cambridge: Cambridge University Press.

Unger, Peter. 1975, *Ignorance*, Oxford: Oxford University Press.

Watson, Gary. 2003, *Free Will*, Oxford: Oxford University Press.

Van Inwagen, Peter. 1975, "Creatures of Fiction," *American Philosophical Quarterly*, Vol. 14, No. 4, pp. 299–308.

Van Inwagen, Peter. 2014, *Metaphysics*, New York: Routledge.

Van Inwagen, Peter. 2017, "Free Will Remains a Mystery," in *Thinking About Free Will*, Cambridge: Cambridge University Press.

Wierenga, Edward. 2016, *The Philosophy of Religion*, Hoboken: Wiley-Blackwell.

Zagzebski, Linda. 1991, *The Dilemma of Freedom and Foreknowledge*, Oxford: Oxford University Press.

Zagzebski, Linda. 2009, *On Epistemology*, Belmont: Wadsworth.

Zimmerman, Dean. 2004, "The Privileged Present: Defending an A-Theory of Time," in Sider et al.

INDEX